Successful Outcomes of Sexual Orientation Change Efforts (SOCE)

An Annotated Bibliography

James E. Phelan, MSW, Psy.D

To order additional copies visit:
www.createspace.com/4575034

DEDICATION

John H. Miller, with much gratitude for your sacrifices and dedication. You were a father to the fatherless.

CONTENTS

"*Success* is getting what you want. Happiness is
wanting what you get"

\- Dale Carnegie

1 INTRODUCTION

This is a comprehensive review of the literature documenting successful outcomes of therapeutic efforts aimed at changing clients' homosexual behaviors, attractions, identification, and/or feelings to various degrees of heterosexual adaptations. Having reviewed many reports, the author has attempted to include a discussion of measurements used, type of treatment or modality of treatment used, sample size, and definition of outcomes, for each one, whenever possible. Outcomes, or success rates, in these cases, have generally been defined by a shift in homosexuality toward heterosexuality either through self-reporting, or through some type of metric. Throughout the years, different paradigms and approaches have been applied to yield various outcomes.

Apart from methodological matters, problems of definitions have made outcome studies complicated to interpret. Specifically, terms such as *sexual orientation* (homosexuality, heterosexuality) and *success* have not always been well defined within the literature. Further, *sexual orientation* as a construct has proven to be wide-ranged, complex, and controversial.

Some advocates of these efforts have claimed that they were helpful to those dissatisfied with their same-gender attractions. While some have agreed that sexuality is not a fixed state, but rather fluid, some critics of therapies aimed at changing sexual orientation claim that they can be harmful and feed into the stigmatization of homosexuality, which was removed from diagnostic criteria as a mental disorder, *per se*, from the American Psychiatric Association's Diagnostic and Statistical Manual (DSM).

While anecdotal accounts have claimed that interventions aimed at changing sexual orientation can be harmful, the body of empirical literature to support those claims is lacking. Largely, however, the treatment of homosexuality has largely evolved from efforts aimed at changing sexual orientation to acceptance and normalization. Therefore, literature on interventions aimed at changing homosexual orientation has progressively become sparse.

However, over the decades there has been literature documenting successful outcomes of efforts aimed at changing homosexual behaviors, attractions, identification, and/or feelings to various degrees of heterosexual adaptations. These paradigms have commonly been referred to as *conversion therapies*, *sexual reorientation therapies*, *reconstructive therapies*, *reparative therapies* (of homosexuality) (Socarides & Kaufman, 1994), and more recently *sexual orientation change efforts* (SOCE) (APA, 2009). The methodology and techniques have varied. Since there is no consensus of what a successful outcome is, each report has maintained independent claims for defining the concept.

Defining Sexual Orientation

Defining terms such as *sexual orientation*, *homosexuality*, and *heterosexuality* have been awkward. *Sexual orientation* is complex, and has not been well defined in the scientific literature (Haldeman, 1994). In a discussion about the definition of *sexual orientation*, Dresher, Stein, and Byne (2005) agreed that it referred to a person's erotic response tendency or sexual attraction, yet realized it was not necessarily binary. Further, they realized that the assessment of one's orientation has several parameters that not only included fantasy, but physiological responses, sexual partners, etc. Further, they distinguished that orientation does not necessarily equivocate sexual identity. For example, they recognized that while one person may have homosexual fantasies, that same person might reject a gay identity. These multifaceted issues make measuring sexual orientation a difficult challenge. Improvements in measuring sexual orientation will rely on improvements in defining the construct comprehensively (Phelan, 2013).

Metrics

A few instruments were used in attempts to measure sexual orientation/preference. Probably the most widely known, is what is commonly referred to as the *Kinsey Scale* [Kinsey's Heterosexual-Homosexual Rating Scale] (Kinsey, Pomeroy, & Martin, 1948). As for the Kinsey Scale, "An individual may be assigned a position on this scale, for each period in his life.... A 7-point scale comes

nearer to showing the many gradations that actually exist"
(Kinsey, et al. 1948, p. 656). The 7-points are:

0	Exclusively heterosexual
1	Predominantly heterosexual, only incidentally homosexual
2	Predominantly heterosexual, but more than incidentally homosexual
3	Equally heterosexual and homosexual
4	Predominantly homosexual, but more than incidentally heterosexual
5	Predominantly homosexual, only incidentally heterosexual
6	Exclusively homosexual.

The Klein Sexual Orientation Grid (KSOG) (Klein,
1978) refined the Kinsey Scale. It remained with 7
intervals, but investigated sexual experience and fantasies
in 3 time frames: The present (the most recent 12 months);
the past (prior to 12 months ago); and the ideal (which is as
close as one can get to intention and prediction of future
behaviors).

Klein included change in people's sexuality over
time. Klein also introduced many different factors that
influenced identity. On the grid, subjects were asked to
consider the following in the present, past, and ideal:

Sexual attraction	To whom are you sexually attracted?
Sexual behavior	With whom do you actually have sex with?
Sexual fantasies	Who do you fantasize about?
Emotional preference	Who do you feel more drawn or close to emotionally?
Social preference	With whom do you like to socialize?
Lifestyle preference	In which community do you prefer to spend your time? In which do you feel most comfortable?
Self-identification	How do you label or identify yourself?

Other measures used included: Bancroft Scores (Bancroft, 1969), Homosexual and Heterosexual Interest Scores (Feldman & MacCulloch, 1971), plethysomography (Freund, 1967; McConaghy, 1967), Scale 5 (Sexual Behavior Ratings) of The Minnesota Multiphasic Personality Inventory (MMPI) (Birk, et al, 1970), Sexual Attraction Scale (Spitzer, 2003; Karten, 2006), Sexual Orientation Method (Feldman, MacCulloch, Mellor, & Pinschof, 1966), Sexual Orientation Self-identity Scale (Spitzer, 2003), and consumer or clinical reports. The latter most commonly used, especially in psychoanalytical reports.

Defining Successful Outcomes

In terms of defining treatment success, Glover (1960) established 3 categories:

Cure	The abolition of conscious homosexual impulses and development of full extension of heterosexual impulse.
Much improved	The abolition of conscious homosexual impulses without development into *full* extension of heterosexual impulse.
Improved	Increased ego integration and capacity to control homosexual impulses.

Karten (2006) defined treatment success as:

- increased sexual feelings and behaviors towards the opposite sex,
- decreased sexual feelings and behaviors towards the same sex,
- a stronger heterosexual identity; or
- improvement in psychological well being.

Therefore, *success* was not always synonymous with

complete *cure*, or complete abolishment of homosexuality. As in the example of Karten (2006), meeting other psychosocial criteria was significant for success, rather then complete abolition of homosexuality. This is, however, contrary to Glover's definition of *cure*, in which a complete abolition of homosexual impulse, hence behavior, therefore seemed to define *success*.

Others saw success simplistically in other directions, for example in sexual performance only, as in the study by Conrad and Wincze (1976) who treated 3 male homosexuals with masturbatory conditioning (orgasmic reconditioning) whereas the 3 men were pleased with being able to perform with women and no longer reported a need for male sexual partners. Thus, the study was considered successful based on a behavioral response only.

Bieber (1967) in discussing success considered "reversal" of "exclusively homosexuality" to "exclusively heterosexuality" (p. 972) as a possibility. In some cases, complete heterosexual orientation with no "sporadic homosexual episodes" was achieved as was reported for 30% of a sample, after a 5-year follow-up. It was assumed this included not only behaviors, but also attractions, identification, and feelings collectively.

As mentioned previously, each study held independent

claims for defining outcomes of treatment. For example, according to Cappon (1965), for all intents and purposes, *cure* represented that the male patient's homosexual activity ceased, heterosexual enjoyment increased (both in erotic perception and value), he had detached from his mother, he had found an ideal father object in the therapist, fantasies were of heterosexual objects, and aggression had been released and used effectively.

Outcomes in the Literature

Changes in sexual orientation from homosexual to heterosexual have been documented in the literature using psychoanalysis, hypnosis, behavior therapies, cognitive therapies, sex therapies, group therapies, pharmacology, spontaneous healing, combination therapies, and others. In the following chapters, I have attempted to include for each, a discussion of: measurements used; type of treatment or modality of treatment used; sample size; and definition of outcomes whenever possible. Bibliography is annotated in sections, chronologically and in format according to the *Publication Manual of the American Psychological Association (6th Edition)*.

2 PSYCHOANALYSIS

Traditionally, psychoanalytic-based therapy with homosexuals who sought to change their sexual orientation mirrored as described by Rubinstein (1958), whereas the patient was assisted to explore causal and contributory factors insomuch that he could obtain intellectual insight and better understand his condition. Commonly, the focus was on strengthening the ego and diminishing inhibition and repressions which where believed to derail heterosexual development. Many analysts felt that therapeutic alliance and working through transference was the golden ticket to repair the wounded oedipal complex for which was believed to be contributory to the condition. The analysis of early development was said to bring to light the vicissitudes of the oedipal complex.

In speaking of the course of analytic treatment of homosexuality, Lorand (1956) identified homosexual desires as perversion, which in the manifest stage, was merely a defense and flight from the patient's deepest desire, which was heterosexuality. Some analysts felt that the flight from heterosexuality, in some men, was an unconscious attempt to avoid incestuous desires (Feldman, 1956; Lorand, 1956). As they saw it, homosexuality was as a defense-structure over the biological determined male-to-female natural foundation.

It is fitting to start the review of psychoanalytic literature with it's said, *father* – Sigmund Freud. Freud (1920a,b) never provided statistical data on outcomes of treatment of homosexuals who sought orientation change, but did note both possibility and pessimism. As for the former, he noted that he had found success possible under specific favorable conditions and noted restoration was only to bisexual functioning. As for the latter, he said that the removal of homosexuality was, in his experience, never an easy matter. Once, a mother asked him if her son's sexual orientation could be changed, and he told her it was possible, but at the same time, not necessary (Freud, 1951).

In a case presented by Gordon (1930), he described an outcome of a male patient who on the onset of treatment, "heterosexuality was repugnant to him [and] there was not even the least desire to seek companionship of females" (p.

154). The patient had homosexual desires and had acted on them on occasion. Gordon used psychoanalytic therapy and techniques which included letter writing and encouragement in making new acquaintances After such, the patient made "no attempt on his part to look for an opportunity of returning to [homosexual] behavior" (p. 155). Eventually, the patient met a woman and "he became undeniably heterosexual" and "an aversion for homosexuality rapidly developed" (p. 155). He finally married and, "...no reference was made by him on his former morbid condition" (p. 155). The duration of treatment was not said, however it was assumed to be long-term as Gordon mentioned he started work with the patient during his time in medical school and continued working with him long distance during his internship (18 months) up until he became a full-pledged physician. After termination of treatment, he mentioned following up with him, "once or twice a year" (p 155), and that, "the adjustment was perfect...he is now a father of two children and very happy in his domestic life" (p. 155).

Stekel (1930) reported 4 cases of *success* with the use of psychoanalysis applied in duration of 2-3 months. Stekel did not use a measure to identify sexual orientation pre or post-therapy, and was not very clear on what success meant for each case, only mentioning that, "in the last year, four of my homosexual patients [had] married and [were] extremely happy" (p. 443).

Anna Freud (1968) in 1952, described 4 patients whom were exclusively homosexual at the onset of psychoanalytical treatment with her. In one outcome, the patient "became heterosexual, a successful husband and father" (p. 389) after becoming conscious that his passive homosexual practices served only to reduce anxiety over his unconscious aggressive urges which ultimately served to defend against destructive wishes toward females. Anna Freud said that when such interpretations were made, "many homosexuals lose some of their fear of women and become able to approach them [romantically]" (p. 251). She told of one other outcome whereas, "[the patient] became heterosexual…married and had children." She said, "Interpretation of the origins of his projections of masculinity had to come first and enable him to reassume his phallic properties. Then, of course, male partners lost their importance and he became able to do without them" (p. 391). Finally, her discussions of the data on the other 2 patients were not indicative of any particular outcome.

London and Caprio (1950) presented two cases of men who, on the onset of psychoanalysis, identified as exclusively homosexual. For the first case, the patient's outcome of the therapy, which included dream interpretations, was described as successful in that he "achieved a greater sense of sexual maturity than he had prior to analysis" (p. 55). He stopped homosexual activity, and found a suitable partner of the opposite sex who he desired to marry. His other symptoms, which were psychosomatic in nature, were also relieved. The course of therapy was approximately 6 months. In the second case, with the course of therapy being much longer, the homosexuality of a man was resolved "by a dissolution of the conflict, by redirecting the instinctive desires which have no intelligence or reasoning powers into normal channels, in other words, by diverting these forces to heterosexuality" (p. 66). A true outcome was harder to distinguish for the second case considering his sexuality was ambiguous from the onset and the fact that there was little data on his progress.

Allen (1952) recorded 2 cases of overt homosexuals (1 male, 1 female), whereas both where "completely cured" (p. 139). By *cured* he meant, "If by treatment he [or she] [was] weaned from [practicing homosexual behaviors] and indulg[ed] in sexual behavior with one of the opposite sex" (p. 139) he or she was cured. The male patient was seen for only 4 consults, which he said, was enough to "unearth the fear at the bottom of his aversion to women" (p. 141). As for the female patient, she too was treated briefly, and after a few visits, she discovered that her hostility and avoidance of men was a reaction to her father. After this discovery and resolution, she gave up lesbianism and engaged to be married to a man whom she was sexually excited by. The latter was not possible prior to treatment.

Caprio (1954) agreed that lesbianism, in and of itself, could be cured through the psychoanalytic process, which helped patients change personality patterns and eliminated mental blocks that stood in their way of heterosexual adjustment. Caprio said, "Many patients of mine, who were former lesbians, have communicated long after treatment was terminated…that they are convinced they will never return to a homosexual way of life" (p. 299). Caprio, while discussing his clinical work with "former lesbians," never formally presented statistical data.

Bergler (1956) claimed that patients could be "cured" once they understood how they were "reduplicating [their] own defense mechanism" (p. 187), by analyzing the "masochistic substructure" (the theory that homosexuals had an unconscious wish to suffer, gratified with self-created "trouble-making") (p. 9), and by working out transference and resistance through the psychoanalytic process. In nearly 30 years of practice, he "successfully concluded analyses of one hundred homosexuals" (p. 188). *Cures* affected 90% of those cases in which the analyst and patient took tremendous time and effort to get to the root of the difficulty (TIME, 1956). Information about follow up was not provided. On average, therapy lasted from 1 to 2 years, with a minimum of 3 appointments each week, per patient. *Cured* meant a lack of interest in the same sex, normal sexual enjoyment (with opposite sex object), and definite characterlogical changes (Bergler, 1956).

Eidelberg (1956) discussed his analysis with a male patient whom he treated for 3 years. As a result, he reported that the patient, "changed considerably...his sexual interest in men and his fear of woman had disappeared" (p. 279). He reported that he helped the patient uncover his unconscious breast envy and that, for the patient, men had represented breastless women. The penis of others was an unconscious way to get the breast he was deprived of. The analysis was said to be successful once the patient was able to destroy the illusion of his "infantile omnipotence" (p. 280).

Albert Ellis (1956) said that those who engaged in psychoanalytically oriented psychotherapy could be "distinctly helped to achieve a satisfactory heterosexual orientation" (p. 194), if they wanted to. That goal applied to 50% of a sample he analyzed. In that sample of 40 individual cases, it was concluded that 18 men and 12 women had outcomes of either "distinct or considerable improvement" (p. 192). This meant they began to lose their fears of the other sex, to enjoy effective heterosexual relations, and to lose their obsessive thoughts about, or compulsive actions concerning homosexuality. Not all patients were exclusively identified as homosexual prior to treatment, as 6 of the men and 6 of the women had moderate or considerable heterosexual activity prior to treatment, whereas the rest had little or none. Ellis (1952) had originally felt that *cure* meant the resolution of exclusive homosexuality, not to exclusive heterosexuality, but to "unneurotically bisexual in desires" (p. 137).

An unpublished report of the Central Fact-Gathering Committee of the American Psychoanalytic Association in 1956 stated that of those analytic patients who completed treatment, 8 were cured and 13 were improved. Another 16 who did not complete treatment were also considered improved. In all reported cures, follow-up communications indicted assumption of full heterosexual role and functioning. Outcome terms were in accordance to those used by Glover (1960) (Socarides, 1968, 1978).

Using the Kinsey Scale, Curran and Parr (1957), in a follow-up study of 59 patients in private analytic practice, found that 9 patients "reported less intense homosexual feelings, or increased capacity for heterosexual arousal" (p. 799). Only one of these patients was diagnosed as exclusively homosexual at the onset of treatment. Treatment "consist[ed] of a mixture of physical, psychological, social, and environmental measures in varying proportions according to the case" (p. 799).

As reported in Berg and Allen (1958)[1], Dr. Clifford Allen conducted psychoanalysis with men based on several theoretical treatment parameters: explanation and education, manipulation of environment, suggestion (including hypnosis and persuasion), superficial analysis, deep transference analysis, conditioning, and sublimation. Patients were taught to suppress shyness and look to women as sexual objects. They were taught that their fear of women stemmed from earlier mothering, though not invariably, and their lacking of male aggressive outlets. Therapy assisted them with providing courage to grow familiar with the opposite sex, using the paradox that "the appetite comes from eating" (p. 70). It took a year or more

[1] Data also reported in Allen (1956) and Allen (1958).

for patients to progress from the superficial transference to deep transference analysis. Allen said, "It definitely is not true that homosexuality is incurable" (p. 104) and discussed 14 cases of apparent *cures*. Cures were discussed as particular to each case ranging from complete attraction change, as in the case where a male patient, homosexual identified from the onset, married a women, whom he became "sexually adjusted" to, and at the termination of therapy "…lost all attraction to other men" (p. 77), to less exclusive changes as in the case where the patient "…was normally sexual with a girl, but admitted that he had had occasional homosexual dreams" (p. 77).

Allen said that "…since his heterosexuality [became] so much stronger than his homosexuality…it was felt that this could be regarded as a cure" (p. 80). He concluded by saying, "Obviously from such a small number of cases no statistical conclusions can be drawn. Nevertheless, these sample cases are typical of others in my long experience with the …treatment of homosexuality" (p. 104).

Hadfield (1958), who conducted treatment with patients over a 30-year period, discussed 9 men whom he claimed were *cured* of homosexuality. Treatment courses varied and therapy was based on the theoretical notion that homosexuality originated not constitutionally, but rather on factors that were psychological and developmental in nature. Patients were not always exclusively homosexual, but those that had histories of heterosexual intercourse were said only be able to so by virtue of homosexual fantasies. *Cured* meant "[the patient lost] his propensity to his own sex and his sexual interests [were] directed towards those of the opposite sex" (p. 1323). He was vivid in noting that *cure* did not mean that these men were just able to manage self-control. Four dated cases were followed-up by Hadfield who claimed they, "were completely cured…with no further episodes" (p. 1324). Their successes were attributed to them having been able to "discover the causes of their disorder in early childhood" (p. 1324).

Robertiello (1959) wrote an entire book dedicated to the discussion of one female homosexual patient, who after analysis with free association and dream interpretation, led to oedipal resolution and her awareness of her unconsciousness assumption that the penis was damaging. Her lesbianism was also discovered, through analysis, to be a "cover up [for] her competitiveness with other women" (p. 250). Her feelings about sexual relationships between men and women became ill after having witnessed parental intercourse as a child. He reported that after several years of analysis she was able to convert to a "mild heterosexual experience." After that, which was said to be "the catalyst" for her change, and in "conjunction with her understanding of her childhood distortions… [it] enabled her to give up homosexuality" (p. 253). After a 2-year follow-up, he reported that she "never once returned to homosexual activity" (p. 253).

Beukenkamp (1960) reported the case of a male patient whom he treated with classic psychoanalytic therapy and later combined with group analysis for a total of 3 ½ years. At the onset of treatment, the patient was exclusively homosexual. Following the start of group work, he noted the patient reduced homosexual behaviors. During the second year of combined treatment, he began to date the opposite sex and "midway in [that] year he was finally able to report that his homosexual behavior had ceased entirely" (p. 285).

Glover (1960) reported that at the end of treatment, 36 out of 81, or 44% of male patients "no longer experienced homosexual impulses and achieved discretion and conscious control" (p. 236). The duration of treatment varied from 5 months to 5 years. The focus of treatment was primarily aimed toward social anxiety and uncovering and releasing inhibiting anxieties towards heterosexuality.

Glover noted that the effectiveness of treatment depended on how the homosexual object choice could be uncovered and the degree in which ego-difficulties could be overcome, how frustrations could be offset, and the degree on which transference rapport could be established and analyzed.

Monroe and Enelow (1960) treated, by way of classic psychoanalysis with free association, 7 male patients who on the onset were described as "homosexual"; that is, they met Kinsey Scale criteria of 4 or 5, whereas any prior heterosexual activity was minimal. Lengths of treatment ranged from 3 to 18 months, and follow-up with 4 patients continued for at least 5 years after termination. Theoretical orientation for treatment was based on classical psychoanalytic theory, which explained homosexuality as a deviation that originated from constitutional, developmental assumptions. Three out of the 7 cases led to considerable success. In one case, the patient's successful outcome was that he avoided previous destructive homosexual activity. The other, "overcame his impotency…and discontinued most of his homosexual soliciting" (p. 484); while the last, at the 5-year follow-up, via letter, revealed, "…he is now married, has a child, and apparently is happy in this setting" (p. 485).

Bieber, et al. (1962), in a 9-year comprehensive study of homosexual men, used an analyst team of 77 members, and provided information on two samples consisting of 106 homosexuals who undertook psychoanalysis. They concluded that 29 out of 106, or 27%, completing treatment became exclusively heterosexual (Kinsey score of 0). From the onset of treatment, 14 of these men were exclusively homosexual, and 15 were predominately homosexual but had heterosexual activity in their histories. Because many different analysts had treated the patients, it was difficult to determine the exact approach taken in treatment other than the broad generalization that they were treated by psychoanalysis. However, it was later explained that psychoanalysis was viewed "as a way of delineating and evaluating irrational beliefs and belief systems associated with fears of injury that [gave] rise to symptoms and functional disturbances" (I. Bieber & T. Bieber, 1979, p. 416). It was said that once those beliefs were attenuated or extinguished, functional abilities opened up.

Bieber (1967) reported that in a 5-year follow-up of patients from the original study, 15 of the 29 had maintained contact with their analyst. Of those 15 cases, 12 had remained exclusively homosexual (Kinsey sore of 0) while 3 reported being predominantly heterosexual with sporadic homosexual episodes under situations of stress. It was explained that most of the patients in treatment did not become heterosexual, but benefited in improved self-esteem, social relationships, assertiveness, and work effectiveness. It was stated that, "A shift to heterosexuality does not mean that the potential for homosexual arousal has been totally extinguished, though in some cases this does occur. Should a post-analytic patient be faced with a recurrence of homosexual interest, he may short-circuit it by identifying the situation that has triggered anxiety about heterosexuality" (I. Bieber & T. Bieber, 1979, p. 419).

Well over a decade after the Bieber, et al. (1962) study, it was reported by I. Bieber and T. Bieber (1979) that they had seen well over 1,000 male homosexuals and "the data obtained [was] in accord with the research findings, thus strengthening its validity and reliability" (p. 417). Without giving specific numbers, they reported, "we have followed patients for as long as 20 years who have remained exclusively heterosexual. Reversal rates now range from 30% to an optimistic 50%" (p. 416).

Coates (1962) examined 45 cases of "homosexual patients" (p. 177) who were treated at The Portman Clinic between the years of 1954 to 1960. The modality of therapy was assumed to be psychoanalytic as clinicians from that clinic were "either psychoanalysts or analytically oriented" (p. 181). Specific courses of treatment and interventions were not detailed in the report. In terms of outcome, he found that 7 out of the 45 cases were classified as "better" (p. 180) meaning having no active homosexual behaviors; however, there may still have been some homosexual fantasies present in some of the cases. Unlike many other studies, this study looked at the extent for which clients were homosexual. This ranged from men who had no sex with other men, but had same-sex fantasies and who had had some heterosexual experiences, to men who had many homosexual liaisons. The former were found more likely to have been later classified as "better" in terms of treatment outcome. Follow-up was indicated in some of the cases. For one, after a 4-year review the patient was still reportedly *better*. Another was followed-up after one year, and he had no homosexual activity, and then two and a half years later he was, "very happy and [was] getting married" (p. 187). It was said in one other narrative that a patient, after 3 years of treatment, was "able to have successful heterosexual intercourse. Shortly after treatment ended, he married and all seemed to be well" (p. 188).

Ovesey, Gaylin, and Hendin (1963) reported

successfully treating 3 men who had some homosexual inclinations, and followed them as long as 5 years, reporting that they were able to maintain pleasurable heterosexual behavior - the goal of therapy. One patient, after a 4-year follow-up had some homosexual fantasies after a business crisis, but it turned out to be transitory and after an additional year he was in remission of homosexual fantasies and behaviors. The approach to treatment was to help the patient understand the unconscious motivational factors to homosexual behavior (e.g. dependency, power) and to break up those circles, thus reversing the homosexual pattern, and therefore establishing heterosexual relations.

Cappon (1965) reported that he treated, "some 200 homosexual patients from a population of 2,000 psychiatric patients" (p. 283). Of his male patients, he presented a 50% *cure* rate. *Cure* meant that these patients changed in respect to their inward tendency toward homosexual acting out behaviors. He noted that 1 in 5 male patients ceased all homosexual behavior as a result of treatment. For his female patients, he presented a success rate of 20%. His success rates also encompassed patients who had "marked improvement" (p. 266). Marked improvement meant that the patient had a positive attitude toward treatment, and a demand for, and optimistic about, the possibility of cure. It was not clear how many patients of the 200 were males, and how many were female.

Mayerson and Lief (1965) conducted a follow-up study of 19 patients (14 males and 5 females) who had originally identified with "homosexual problems" (p. 331). The mean duration of analytic-based therapy was 1.7 years, and the mean interval between end of therapy and the follow-up was 4.5 years. In the overall evaluation at the time of follow-up, 47% of patients were found to be "apparently recovered" or "much improved" and identified as "exclusively heterosexual". Twenty-two percent of them had originally identified as "exclusively homosexual." In addition to sexual identity, factors included in the overall evaluation considered improved psychosomatic and psychological adjustments, social relationships, and depth of insight.

Hadfield (1966) reported 2 more cases of "cure" (p. 678). In both cases, the patients were said to be practicing homosexuals, and they had "no sexual attraction at all to the opposite sex" (p. 678). In one case, after discovering that his homosexuality was based in his fear of women, and being successfully analyzed he, "happily married with a child [and] all repulsions [to women went away]" (p. 678).

In the other case, in which the essential feature was also fear of women, "as a result of his analysis he was cured and became heterosexual not only in his waking life but – what is more significant – in his dreams" (p. 678).

Mintz (1966) reported using the combination of individual and group psychoanalysis for 2 or more years whereas 3 of 10 men who identified as exclusively homosexual reported "satisfactory heterosexual adjustment" (p. 193). She described them as such: "Two are enjoying heterosexuality and report freedom of conflict" and "one [who was still in treatment at the time] has lost interest in homosexuality and enjoys satisfying heterosexual relationships" (p. 194). The criteria for successful outcome included: the patients were able to become conscious of heterosexual defenses; they developed a stronger sense of personal identity through contact with heterosexual men and women; they dealt with anxieties and avoidance of women; and, they made corrective emotional responses that led to greater self-esteem.

Kaye, et al. (1967) polled more than 150 psychoanalysts who treated female homosexual patients in their practice, and received back 24 completed 26-page surveys. Eight of the 15 cases that were reported to be in the "homosexual range" (Kinsey scores of 4-6), shifted to a

Kinsey score of 0 (exclusively heterosexual) at the termination of treatment, or when the analyst filled out the survey. They concluded by saying, "Apparently at least 50% of them can be helped by psychoanalytic treatment" (p. 633).

Socarides (1968) described in detail his psychoanalytical work with a male patient who was able to find "stabilization toward heterosexuality" and to be "able to express himself heterosexually" (p. 135), while at the onset of therapy he identified exclusively homosexually oriented. Success was ultimately measured in that he had resolved his fears of incest with his mother. In a second case, he described another man who on the onset of therapy identified exclusively homosexually oriented, but through the course of psychoanalytic therapy was able "to enjoy the company of a young woman with whom he had his first heterosexual intercourse" (p. 155). This patient was not said to become exclusively heterosexual since "homosexual images would sometimes intrude" (p. 155). The outcome of the therapy was not measured, however, by his shift in orientation, but by the analytic process that lead him to discover his masochism for which he had been playing the passive controller of others.

A female homosexual, whom Socarides treated for a 4-

year period, also reported a shift toward heterosexuality. On the onset of treatment she was considered fully homosexual, but "during the course of treatment, heterosexual interests had been observed and one time - approximately the third year of treatment - she felt strong affectionate interest in a male" (p. 193). In all cases, Socarides took the stance that homosexuality was an anxiety-ridden solution, and that once anxieties were analyzed and resolved, patients' homosexual contacts became less needed and they were potentially capable of seeking an opposite sex love object. Socarides (1978) reported that from the periods of 1967 to 1977, 20 out of 44 patients (one being female), nearly 50%, treated by him using "full-scale psychoanalysis" had developed full "heterosexual functioning" to include "love feelings for their heterosexual partners" (p. 406).

Jacobi (1969), in his practice, treated 60 patients as having "all different types and degrees of homosexuality" (p. 52). Examples of such ranged from "overt" (those who practiced homosexual behaviors via the anus) to "spiritual union between two men" (p. 49). Out of the 60 patients treated, 6 or 10% made a "transformation to heterosexuality" (p. 53). While he did not directly explain what he meant by his assertion, he was clear in his writing that heterosexuality equated to "heterosexual relationships" or the patient "finding [his] way to a woman." He distinguished that patient subset from one that lived in a "split state" (e.g. in a heterosexual relationship, yet still had homosexual tendencies). Those who made a "transformation to heterosexuality" were not described as the latter.

Lamberd (1969) believed that in a limited number of cases, male homosexuality could be successfully treated by psychoanalysis with a direct attack on the symptoms of phobic avoidance of women. This included active encouragement of heterosexual contacts, exploration of anxiety, and explorations of attitudes and fears of women. He cited 3 case histories in which this approach had successful outcomes. Therapeutic process was also attributed to positive transference of patient to therapist who was "firm, strong, and nonthreatening" (p. 517). In the first case, the patient was without overt homosexual acting out, but had fantasies and dreams. After 150 hours of treatment, "he completely overcome his phobic avoidance of women and redirected his sexual desires [to women]" (p. 515). The patient in the second case was said to be exclusively homosexually oriented, with no heterosexual contacts in his history. After 60 hours of treatment, "his homosexual desires, fantasies, and dreams completely disappeared and [he had] a satisfactory marital and sexual adjustment" (p. 516). In the third case, the patient had been married, but was impotent with his wife and had a long history of homosexual activity. After 12 months of treatment, at an 18-month follow-up he, "was completely heterosexual, with no homosexual impulses, dreams, or fantasies. [In addition], he had become more assertive and aggressive" (p.517).

According to Ovesey (1969), a successful outcome for men in treatment to change sexual orientation from homosexuality to heterosexuality was not just "potency" with women, but "total relationship" to include marriage (p. 123-124). He reported 3 successfully treated males with follow-up of 5 or more years. Treatment focused on understanding unconscious motives that had impelled the patients to flee from women and seek contact with men. After such, insight "facilitat[ed] reversal of a homosexual pattern and...establish[ed]...heterosexuality" (p. 154).

Wallace (1969) reported "successful treatment" (p. 263) of a man with ego-dystonic homosexuality, who had a history of one incidence of heterosexual coitus. At the end of a total of 88 hours of psychoanalytic-based therapy covering eight-and-a-half months, the patient "achieved a heterosexual image of himself and shortly afterwards married" (p. 364). *Success* did not include heterosexual activity only, but also included strengthened ego functions and insights into his fears of heterosexuality, as well as uncovering some of the unconscious fantasies in the homosexual encounters. In the latter, for example, "he had been looking for a substitute for his father in his homosexual relationships" (p. 349).

Siegel (1988) described what she referred to as "the most comprehensive clinical investigation [of female homosexuality]…derive[ed] from the largest sample (12) of female homosexuals treated by a single psychoanalyst" (p. xv of *Foreword*). As an outcome of treatment, half of the women became "fully heterosexual." On the onset of treatment, these women saw themselves as exclusively homosexual (strove for same-sex liaisons, had homoerotic fantasies only). The phases of analytic therapy used included ideal mother transference; hypochondriacal preoccupation; denial of the need for a mother; body image projections; analyst interjected fantasizes; homosexual actions as a defense against aggression transference; and complete working through of transference. Siegel did not set out with the goal of changing sexual orientation, *per se*; therefore, no set parameters for change were identified. It so happened to be a result, as self-reported by half of her cases. According to Siegel, successful treatment was met when transference was finally resolved, regardless if orientation had changed or not.

Berger (1994) described 2 cases of treatment success. One case, "resulted in the patient marrying and fathering three children and living a heterosexually fulfilling and enjoyable life" (p. 255). The other was a "successful long-term psychodynamic psychotherapy treatment [which] helped relieve the patient of his original presenting symptoms and enabled him to become comfortably and consistently heterosexual" (p. 255).

Finally, a survey of 285 anonymous members of the American Psychoanalytic Association conducted by MacIntosh (1994) reported that out of 1,215 homosexual patients analyzed by those members, 23% "changed to heterosexuality from homosexuality" (p. 1203). As in the study by Bieber, et al. (1962), considering so many analysts were involved, it was difficult to determine the exact approach taken per each patient in treatment other than the broad generalization that they were treated by psychoanalysis in general

3 COGNITIVE AND BEHAVIORAL THERAPIES

The goals of cognitive behavioral therapists were not directly the same as those of psychoanalysts. The latter had concerns of getting to the root of problems and resolving oedipal conflict and defenses, while the former generally focused on behavioral changes only. Cognitive therapists focused on changing behaviors through changing negative, faulty, or otherwise irrational thinking patterns. Behavioral-based therapies not only have been used to treat unwanted homosexual behavior, but also used to treat, with said success, a variety of sexual conditions such as, impotence, frigidity, voyeurism, exhibitionism, transvestism, and fetishism (Rachman, 1961).

Behavioral therapists have generally worked under the notion that there is no such unitary thing as "homosexuality" (Birk, 1980, p. 376). Aversion therapies aimed to change sexual behaviors were used as early as the 1930s (Max, 1935), but due to ethics concerns are now abolished from practices. The goals of aversion therapy were to induce an aversion (e.g. by way of shock, apomorphine injections, exposure to odors/chemicals) to previously attracted same-sex persons usually with the pairing of a complementary attempt (usually by projectory slides) to increase attraction to the opposite sex. In classical methods of conditioning, the repeated association of an attractive objective with an unpleasant stimulus resulted in aversion to that object (Mather, 1966). Also used, was desensitization, a technique to help patients curve fears to social and heterosexual anxieties. Avoidance conditioning (Wolpe, 1958) was be used to force an aversion to where the homosexuality would be unpleasant, and therefore avoided. Backward conditioning had also been used (McConaghy & Barr, 1973). Covert sensitization (Cautela, 1996) was introduced so that the stimuli was imagined only, followed by a build up of an avoidance to the homosexual stimuli. Davison and Wilson (1973) polled over 200 behavioral therapists and found a mean of 60% claimed success in treating homosexual behavior using the various techniques described above. Birk (1980) was under the impression that merging psychoanalytic and behavioral paradigms could bring about successful outcomes. For example, while a psychoanalyst could help unravel oedipal conflicts, a behaviorist could train in assertiveness, for example, whereas to facilitate meaningful communication between the patient and his emotionally distant father.

Poe (1952), by use of 65 sessions of adaptational therapy (Rado, 1949), treated a 40-year-old man who practiced homosexuality for 22 years. Adpatational therapy viewed homosexuality as an adaption, which after insight, could be changed. As a result of this therapy, with this patient, it was reported "men [no longer] appeared sexually attractive" (p. 32) to him, and he ceased his homosexual behavior and married. Poe noted that not only did the patient make a behavioral change, but a "psychodynamic altercation" (p. 23) because the patient's whole mental "frame of reference" (p. 23) changed. He not only stopped having sex with men, he stopped finding them attractive.

Albert Ellis (1959) described a case of a 35 year-old man who came to therapy as exclusively homosexual seeking to develop heterosexual interests. The goal was not necessarily to reduce all homosexual desires or activities, but to have him overcome blocks to heterosexuality as much as to create heterosexual desires and activities (enjoy sex with females). Ellis, said, "Once he overcame [irrational blocks against heterosexuality] and actively desired and enjoyed sex relationships with females, it would be relatively unimportant from a mental health standpoint whether he still had homosexual leanings as well" (p. 339). Ellis reported that the patient stopped homosexual behavior and "began to be sexually and emotionally successful with females" (p. 342). After a 3-year follow-up, "he [was] completely disinterested in homosexual relations" (p.343) and "was getting along nicely in marriage" (p. 343). He concluded:

> As [the patient] began to change fundamental irrational beliefs that motivated his homosexuality and neurotic behavior, the client's symptoms almost automatically began to disappear and he was able to change from a fixed, exclusive homosexual to a virtually hundred per cent heterosexually oriented individual. (p. 343)

Shealy (1972) reported that an exclusive homosexually identified male patient changed because of the application of Rational Therapy, combined with other behavioral techniques. As an outcome of 15 hours of therapy, "the patient reported that his overt homosexual behavior had been completely eliminated and that his erotic images had dropped to about 25 percent of the before-treatment amount" (p. 221).

Freund (1960) treated homosexually active patients using chemical aversion and technique slides. After a 3-year follow-up in a non-forensic patient sample, he found 12 who had shown long-term heterosexual behavior. In a second follow-up, after 2 more years, he found that none of them could claim a complete absence of homosexual desires, but 6 claimed complete absence of homosexual behaviors. Success was seen because of an increase in heterosexual behaviors, rather than a decrease in homosexual desires.

Stevenson and Wolpe (1960), by use of assertiveness training, reported that 2 homosexuals established heterosexual behavior. In the most striking case, the patient had been behaviorally homosexual since puberty (for 8-years) and his underassertiveness was most pronounced in dealing with his stepfather. In 10 hours of treatment with emphasis on assertiveness and power with his stepfather, change came in the way of a personality shift and heterosexual shift. He was able to marry and had a child. The same outcome was confirmed at a 3 and 4-year follow-up.

B. James (1962), by use of aversion therapy, reported an outcome in which the patient had no self-reported recurrence of homosexuality after an 18-month follow-up (B. James & Early, 1963). The patient in this study initially reported exclusive homosexual desire and behavioral, and at follow-up, he reported exclusive heterosexual desires and behaviors.

Feldman and MacCulloch (1964) produced a preliminary report of their work with a man who desired to change his sexual orientation. He was a practicing homosexual since his teen years. He had a history of some opposite-sex dating but without any erotic involvement. At the onset of treatment, he was rated on the Kinsey Scale as a 5 (predominantly homosexual, only incidentally heterosexual). After 28 sessions of systemic conditioned aversion therapy, he reported a decrease in attractions to men and increased attractiveness to female photographs. Outside the laboratory, he reported a decrease in his homosexual fantasy life and found a girlfriend who he had intercourse with. He reported satisfactory intercourse, with some remaining, "although easily controlled, interest in men" (p. 170). Nine months after the completion of treatment, his post-treatment Kinsey Scale rating was a 1 (predominantly heterosexual, only incidentally homosexual).

Using behavioral techniques, derived from learning theory, Schmidt, Castell, and Brown (1965) reported that out of 16 patients who identified as homosexual, 8 or 50% showed *marked improvement* after discharge. One other patient showed *moderate improvement*. *Marked improvement* meant that the patients had no homosexual behaviors, and *moderate improvement* meant that symptoms were present, but to a lesser degree (e.g. decrease in behavior, but not total decrease). Rating scores from 2 independent raters assessed these patients. The findings were also confirmed after a 1-year follow-up.

Solyom and Miller (1965) treated 6 male homosexuals, all but 1 suffering from anxiety, with the use of a double (differential) conditioning technique in which a projection of a picture of a seminude male was accompanied by an electric shock, while a photograph of a female was positively reinforced by termination of a continuous electric shock. Using plethysmograph response for objective assessment of therapeutic results, no change was found in autonomic responses to male pictures but there was an apparent increase in responses to sexually stimulating female pictures.

Feldman and MacCulloch (1965) reported successful outcome after using anticipatory-avoidance learning technique. They reported that 18 of 25 patients (72%) showed a complete or near-complete absence of homosexual fantasy and were either actively practicing heterosexuality or had strong heterosexual fantasies (follow-up period was between 1-14 months; a mean of 6 months).

Mather (1966) reported that out of 36 patients identified as overt homosexual treated with behavioral and aversion techniques, 25 were considered much improved on the Kinsey Scale. Measurements were taken at the beginning of treatment (length of treatments varied) and ended after 1 year. "Improvement mea[nt] a cessation of homosexual activity either in deed or [fantasy]" (p. 202). Eleven patients who had never had heterosexual intercourse prior to treatment, were reported to do so after treatment.

Cautela (1967) reported a case study of a male patient he treated by use of covert sensitization and desensitization (method used by Wolpe, 1958) at Temple University Medical School. After 4 months of treatment, the patient reportedly, "ha[d] not engaged in any homosexual behavior" (p. 464), which was the goal of treatment. Independent observers in the institution confirmed the findings. Cautela (1967) felt the reason for success was that, through treatment, the patient obtained a sense of control over his own behaviors.

Kraft (1967, 1970) treated 2 overt homosexually identified men (non-heterosexually responsive), with systematic desensitization, and some psychoanalysis, and found that they sexually responded to heterosexual stimuli after treatment, which was the goal and therefore considered successful.

MacCulloch and Feldman (1967) treated 43 men with overt homosexual behaviors with anticipatory avoidance conditioning, over a 3-year period (minimum period for follow-up was 12 months). They reported that 25 of the 36 patients who completed therapy were "significantly improved (14 on Kinsey scale 0; 9 on Kinsey scale 1; and 2 on Kinsey scale 2)" (p. 597).

Serban (1968) presented a case of a male (taken from a series of 25 cases) who was considered homosexual in both "desire and outlook," had both overt and covert homosexual behaviors, and no overt heterosexual behaviors or overt desires. Through use of *existential therapy* (Frankl, 1967), the patient's successful outcome was measured in that he was able to "integrate his sexuality" which gave him a "sense of power, of real equality with others, and more than anything else, a sense of fulfillment of his most secret desire – to be free, to decide on his own whether or not to be homosexual" (p. 501).

Bergin (1969) used the combination of desensitization and self-regulation techniques with two exclusively homosexually identified patients (one male, one female). As for the male patient, after being treated for 20 sessions over a 6-month period, he was successfully desensitized of his fears of women and was able to control any homosexual impulses. Approximately 1-year after treatment he was married and "the marriage appear[ed] to be continuing successfully" (p. 115). Bergin stated that, "[the patient] was followed-up at intervals after treatment and was found to be free of this problem for a two-year period" (p. 115). The female case was also considered to be successful in that after 41 sessions, an 8-month period, she successfully desensitized her fears of men, and was able to control her homosexual impulses. At the 10-month follow-up, she too was successfully married.

Fookes (1969) summarized his clinical experience of 5 years using aversion treatment with 27 cases referred to as "sexual perversions". Success ranged from 60% with homosexuality to 100% with fetishism-transvestism, and no harmful effects of aversion treatments were discernible. The patients were said to have welcomed the changes, which consisted of the loss of desire for the extinqished behaviors.

McConaghy (1969) treated 40 male patients with aversion therapy to reduce homosexuality, whereas following treatment, the patients showed significantly less penile plethysmography responses to homosexual stimuli with no complaints of harm. Changes in penile response were still present at follow-up a year or more later which correlated to earlier responses in treatment (McConaghy, 1970).

Larson (1970), after use of an adaption of Feldman and MacCulloch's (1965, 1971) anticipatory avoidance learning approaches, likewise reported treatment success. He reported that after treatment, patients where able to decrease homosexual behavior and increase heterosexual behavior, however the number of patients in treatment was not clear.

Kendrick & McCullough (1972) reported using a two-phase behavioral treatment plan with a 21-year-old male who wanted to achieve a heterosexual adjustment. The patient's history was primarily homosexual, with only occasional arousal by females. After treatment, he was assessed via clinical observation and the patient's completion of the Reinforcement Survey Schedule (Cautela & Kasternbaum, 1967). The outcomes indicated that, after treatment, he had decreased homosexual urges and increased heterosexual contacts.

McConaghy, Proctor, and Barr (1972) treated 40 male patients with aversion therapy and at 2 weeks following treatment the patients showed significantly less penile plethysmography responses to heterosexual stimuli. The changes in penile volume were reported to correlate with the "reduction in homosexual feelings [they] reported at follow-up 6 months later" (p. 65). Specifically, however in McConaghy's (1970) follow-up study of 40 male patients, more reduced homosexual feelings were noted with the use of apomorphine than with shock techniques. At 2 weeks after treatment, male patients showed significantly more penile volume increase to pictures of women and less penile volume for male pictures, a "more heterosexual type of response" (p. 560).

Bancroft (1970) reported that 5 out of 15, or 33%, of homosexually active men, treated with desensitization made significant shifts toward heterosexual behavior. Hatterer (1970) found in a follow-up of his treatment of 143 homosexually active men, which 49, or 34%, recovered completely; that is, achieved their desired goal of exclusive heterosexual behavior.

Huff, (1970) used desensitization in the treatment of an exclusive homosexual man who said he "[wanted] to be heterosexual", but he had fear and anxiety to pursue this. According to MMPI profiles and scaling of homosexual and heterosexual urges, the patient rated less anxiety toward women, and saw them as less aversive sexual objects, than prior to treatment. He also reported, "he felt less homosexual and began to be sexually aroused to scenes [of the opposite sex] in the desensitization session" (p. 102). Huff made this point about treatment outcome,

> Rogers and Dymond (1954) maintained that in successful therapy the patient's self-concept and ideal self-concept become more alike. They attribute this to insight gained in a supportive, accepting interpersonal relationship. At the beginning of therapy Mr J's self- and ideal self-concepts were very discrepant. When he was re-evaluated at the end of therapy, this large discrepancy no longer existed. (Huff, 1970, p. 102)

Mandel (1970) reported a trial of classical conditioning with 2 male patients. One patient, after 2-months of follow-up (6 sessions), his homosexual behavior and temptations "ceased completely...and he developed a happy relationship with a suitable girl" (p. 94). The other patient increased his efforts to find a woman; his homosexual contacts decreased from 4 to 3, and his heterosexual fantasies increased from 0 to 2 per month.

Using covert sensitization techniques (utilizing imagery to build up an aversion to homosexual behavior), Cautela and Wisocki (1971) reported a 37% success rate (3 out of 8 men treated) after a 1-year follow-up. The success was based on the patient's desire to achieve heterosexual behavior. Success was measured by subjective and objective reports, which stated that exclusive homosexual behavior and urges were in full remission.

Feldman and MacCulloch (1971) worked with 36 homosexually active patients using anticipatory avoidance learning therapy. They reported that 57% achieved heterosexual behaviors after a 1-year follow-up, which was their desired outcome. Feldman, MacCulloch, and Orford (1971) reported follow-up results on research done between the years of 1963-1965 with 63 male patients who were homosexually active. They reported that 29% of the patients who had no prior heterosexual experience had changed. Change was indicated by the cessation of homosexual behavior, only occasional homosexual fantasies or attractions, and strong heterosexual fantasy, behavior, or both.

Van den Aardweg (1971) reported that 9 out of 20 patients treated using *exaggeration therapy* (a cognitive-behavioral approach) were completely *cured*, meaning no homosexual fantasies or behaviors were reported.

Hallam and Rachman (1972) administered a course of electrical aversion therapy to 7 patients complaining of "deviant sexual behavior" including homosexual impulses. Four made discernible progress. After treatment, significant changes in heart rate response to sexual stimuli were detected. The successful cases showed a significant increase in the time required to imagine sexual material.

Barlow and Agras (1973) found heterosexual responsiveness increase in 3 subjects after follow-up utilizing fading techniques, measured by penile responses and behavioral reports.

Maletzky and George (1973) reported that 10 homosexually active males who were treated with covert sensitization behavioral therapy were able to achieve heterosexual behavior after a 12-month follow-up.

Utilizing avoidance conditioning, classical conditioning, or backward conditioning, with a randomized sample of 46 homosexually identified men, McConaghy and Barr (1973) reported that at one year following treatment, approximately 50% or 23 patients reported a decrease in heterosexual feelings, and in half an increase in heterosexual feelings. There was no significant difference in efficacy between the 3 forms of treatment used.

Cantón-Dutari (1974, 1976) used desensitization, aversion, and a contraction-breathing technique to help active homosexual men control their arousal to homosexual images. Out of 54 patients, 48 were considered successfully treated as they had attained the primary goal of controlling sexual arousal in the presence of a homosexual stimulus. Forty-four of 49 were able to perform heterosexual intercourse, whereas before that was not possible. Twenty-two were followed for an average of 3-1/2 years. On the Kinsey Scale, 11 of them were rated as exclusively heterosexual, and the other 11 masturbated to homosexual imagery but did not involve themselves in homosexual behavior; 4 of the patients married.

Herman, Barlow, and Agras (1974) studied classical conditioning of sexual response to female stimuli, using slides and homosexually oriented films with 3 homosexually active men by way of a single subject experimental designs. Critical variables in the classical conditioning procedure were systematically introduced and removed while objective and subjective measures of homosexual and heterosexual behavior were recorded (e.g. penile responses and self-reports of sexual urges and fantasies). Clients completed the Sexual Orientation Method (Feldman, et al. 1966) questionnaire before and after each experimental phase. In 2 clients, classical conditioning was an effective procedure for increasing arousal for heterosexual stimulus.

Orwin, James, and Turner (1974) reported treatment success by use of electric aversion therapy for one patient, whereas he reported arousal for heterosexual stimulus and no longer practiced homosexual behavior. Tanner (1974) assigned 8 men, who identified themselves as exclusive homosexuals, to an automated aversive (shock) conditioning group, and eight others to a waiting list control group following a pre-training assessment. At the end of 8 weeks, all subjects participated in a second assessment. The aversive conditioning group showed significant decreases in erectile response to slides of male nudes in self-rated arousal to male slides and on the Masculinity-Femininity Scale (Mf) scale of the Minnesota Multiphasic Personality Inventory (MMPI), while showing significant increases in reports of frequency of sex with women, frequency of socializing with women, and the frequency of sexual thoughts about women versus men.

Freeman and Meyer (1975) used classical behavioral approaches and reported that 7 out of 9, or 78% of patients, who were exclusively homosexual, switched from homosexual behavior to an "exclusive heterosexual orientation" (p. 210) after treatment, at an 18-month follow-up.

Using covert sensitization methods (Cautela, 1967) over a period of several years, Callahan, Krumboltz, and Thoresen (1976) reported that at the 4-1/2 year follow-up point, a subject said he had "no problem with homosexual arousal and that he ha[d] a good sexual relationship with his wife" (p. 244). According to measurement on the Kinsey Scale, he was rated at 1 (predominantly heterosexual). This supported the work of Segal and Sims (1972) who also reported success by using imagery to build up aversion to homosexual behavior in a patient seeking such behavioral changes.

Using systematic desensitization and training in heterosexual skills, Phillips, Fischer, Groves, and Singh (1976) reported a successful behavioral outcome of a male patient. Their definition of success meant that the man was able to initiate heterosexual contact by the 18-month follow-up with no homosexual activity.

Using systemic desensitization, S. James (1978) treated 4 subgroups of men, for a total of 40. Ratings via various scales after 2-yers of extinction, or aversion desensitization were administered. Out of the 40 patients, 15 were *improved* and out of that 15, 6 were "complete[ly] absent of homosexual fantasies, interests, and behaviors [with the] presence of heterosexual fantasies, attractions, and behavior up to successful sexual intercourse" (p. 32). Nine patients were *slightly improved*, meaning they had some increase in heterosexual interest and some diminution of homosexual interest, but not in totality.

Pradhan, Ayyar, and Bagadia (1982) demonstrated that by utilizing behavioral modification techniques, 8 out of 13 male homosexuals showed a shift to heterosexual behavior that was maintained in a 6-month and 1-year follow-up. Van den Aardweg (1986a, 1986b) reported treating over 100 homosexuals using cognitive approaches and found that one-third of them had been *radically changed* to a heterosexual adaptation.

As Throckmorton (1998) discussed, many behavioral experts, largely from the 1970's era, have advocated for the use of a variety of behavioral techniques to achieve sexual shifts toward heterosexuality (Gray, 1970; Marquis, 1970; Blitch & Haynes, 1972; Hanson & Adesso, 1972; Barlow, 1973; Rehm & Rozensky, 1974; Wilson & Davison, 1974; Freeman & Meyer, 1975; Greenspoon & Lamal, 1987; Tarlow, 1989; Barlow & Durand, 1995). Studies of cognitive and behavioral intervention are generally narrow in focus; while they discuss changing sexual behavior, they generally fail to expel data regarding other psychosocial dimensions. The use of aversive therapies (e.g. chemicals, electronic shock, etc.) were popularized, and used successfully, up until the 1970's; not just for the use of changing sexual behavior, but for a variety of behaviors. However, because of advocacy dealing with the ethics of aversion therapy, its use rapidly disappeared.

4 GROUP THERAPIES

Eliasberg (1954) conducted group psychoanalysis by way of dream analysis. He treated 2 groups of 6 men who were on probation, yet their treatment was voluntary. He wrote outcome narratives for 5 cases where success was noted. *Success*, however, varied for each case with no absolute criteria. In all, shifts from homosexual to heterosexual were noted; however, these men had ambiguous sexuality from the onset of treatment as they had been married or had some prior contact with woman, with the exception of one case. For these patients, complete shift of orientation was not the goal or outcome. Rather, outcome was described as:

> a) I feel stronger all around, as to resistance; b) there are fewer relapses; c) I can see from my dreams that I am in a better position to reject those men; d) It comforts me that my interests are shunted away, unconsciously, from homosexuality. (p.224)

The paper only mentioned that one case was followed-up; however, while followed for 3 years, "no trouble was reported" (p. 223).

Hadden (1958) reported that he treated 3 homosexual subjects in groups, with the therapeutic emphasis on breaking down rationalizations that homosexuality was a pattern of life that they wish to follow, by breaking down rationalization that activated anxieties, and ego-strengthening by gaining identification with others in the group. He did not put focus on the nature or frequencies of homosexual experiences. In one case, after treatment of 10 months, the man had initial interests in the opposite sex, began petting with a few females, and started to have erotic heterosexual dreams, which prior to treatment, were exclusively homosexual.

Smith and Bassin (1959) presented 4 cases of men in psychiatric treatment for adult offenders. After about 2 years in treatment, one group member's successful outcome was identified by him undertaking marriage, and another started to have heterosexual intercourse exclusively, where prior to treatment that was not the case. One member showed improvement by lessening anxiety and having a better acceptance of the difference between male and female sex roles, while the other looked for a method of adjustment and acceptance rather than any changes toward heterosexuality. Treatment modality was primarily the *client-centered* approach within a Rogerian frame of reference. The work of Hadden (1957) was also influential to the treatment process.

Litman (1961) reported the outcome of a male patient treated in a group comprised of 4 heterosexual women and 3 heterosexual men. At the onset of treatment he "was openly homosexual in his social life and for the last five years he had been living with a roommate…in a stable homosexual union" (p. 440). He came to therapy because he wanted to break through his feelings of isolation and his difficulty communicating with others. The goal of therapy was not to change sexual orientation. As an outcome however, erotic overtures from the women members and competitive moves by the men evoked nonhomosexual, masculine responses from the patient. His overt homosexuality was interpreted as a character defense, which was often acted out as hostility, and infantile behavior. During therapy his "hostility and his need to erotize and devalue every close relationship decreased" (p. 445). After one year of being discharged from the group he reported back that he was in analytic therapy and was having "an idyllic love affair with a young European woman" (p. 446).

Hadden (1966) reported successful outcomes of his treatment groups with men who identified as exclusively homosexual. Group work was open-ended, held weekly, and was conducted in a dynamically-oriented fashion with emphasis on affect, dream analysis, experiential processes, anxiety activations, probing of the development of early life conflicts, and environment changes. Twelve of 32 patients who had been in treatment for 20 sessions or more, "progressed to an exclusively heterosexual pattern of adjustment" (p. 15). In terms of follow-up, he reported that 5 marriages had taken place "which range[ed] in duration from 15 months to 5-years... [and were] reported as happy" (p. 20).

Birk, Miller, and Cohler (1970) also reported a success rate of one-third claiming that after 2-years of group therapy facilitated by male-female cotherapists, 9 out of 26 overt homosexually identified men "shift[ed] to or towards heterosexuality" (p. 37). This group was said to mirror, and had the specific advantages of, the work done by Hadden (1966). Adding to the successful outcome was the process for which helped men experience a new kind of object relationship with women (through identification with the female therapist), and role modal identification with men (through identification with the male therapist).

Hadden (1971) summed up his group work claiming that, "about one-third of those patients who persist in treatment do reach an effective heterosexual adjustment. In another third improvements occur in other neurotic manifestations and the homosexual pattern is to some degree altered" (p. 127).

T. Bieber (1971) reported outcomes in an unorganized manner. First, she outlined 5 cases and illustrated them; each had a different outcome. However, then in a summary of results she said, "*In toto*, 9 homosexuals have participated in the group described...one exclusively homosexual...shifted to exclusive heterosexuality" (p. 532). Then, she concluded, "the rate of recovery among homosexuals treated in these groups is 40 percent" (p. 532). T. Bieber worked under the notion that homosexuality was a symptomatic reaction to failed oedipal paradigms. Groups were either heterogeneous (mixed with heterosexuals, male and female) or homogeneous (made up entirely of male homosexuals). Although heterogeneous groups allowed men to reveal sexual practices, provide competition among members, see reactions to women, feel part of the group, and work through their transference with a female therapist, homogeneous group work was most desired because it allowed men to be less guarded and allowed them to open up more quickly.

Pittman and DeYoung (1971) treated 10 patients in heterogeneous groups over a 7-year period. Six patients were considered homosexual, however not all were exclusively homosexual. For example, one male patient was bisexual; although he preferred women, his relationships were largely with homosexual men. Three patients were cited to be successful "in the groups, achieving their major goals for change, giving up their homosexual relationships, and finally establishing satisfactory relationships with heterosexual partners" (p. 69). One particular case process was explained in that the patient was able to seduce a woman whom he had been impotent. Later, he married and "he never desired to return to homosexuality and soon became comfortable in marriage" (p. 68). The mixed groups were cited to assist to the successful outcome in that the mixed members (heterosexual men and women) provided support, advice, and acted as role models. Group members stressed discontinuation of homosexual activity, encouraged heterosexual activity, and helped members to explore the reasons behind homosexual desires. For example, one male patient "had overcome the underlying vaginaphobia with support, pressure and detailed advice from heterosexual group members" (p. 70).

Truax and Tourney (1971) conducted a controlled study of male homosexuals in group psychotherapy at the *University of Iowa*. The treatment group consisted of 30 patients, and the control group consisted of 20 untreated subjects. The patient group met for 1.5 hours per week for at least a 7-month period. The therapeutic process helped patients explore and resolve feelings of inferiority, rejection, and over-bondedness with their mothers. The study considered outcomes on a 9-point rating scale from *markedly worse* to *markedly improved*. The latter, of course, was considered the most successful outcome. In specific terms of outcomes, the treatment group showed a decrease [in time devoted to homosexuality] while no such shift was seen in the controls" (p. 709). Other significant marked improvements were in social relations, insight, and ability to concentrate; there were also decreases in neurotic symptoms. Ten patients were evaluated in follow-up of 1-3 years and 8 of them "demonstrated definite clinical improvements" (p. 710). Improvements consisted of increased heterosexual orientation, decreased homosexual preoccupation, reduced neurotic symptomatology, improved social relations, and increased insight into the causes and implications of homosexuality. Changes in sexual behavior included increased heterosexual dates, decreased homosexual experiences, and increased heterosexual intercourse. More improvement was seen in the associated neurotic symptomatology than in the homosexual orientation, although this latter parameter of functioning improved with further therapy.

Birk (1974) reported on the outcome of homosexual or bisexual men who were dissatisfied with their sexual orientation and treated in group psychotherapy led by a male-female co-therapy team. Therapy was said to foster therapeutic insight through associative resonance, and to provide models, support, and reinforcement of new behaviors, such as heterosexual interests and activities, assertiveness, identification with a male via the male therapist, and corrective emotional experience of simultaneous rapport with the male and female therapists. Of the 66 patients treated, 27 remained in treatment for 1.5 years or longer, and 85% of them experienced "at least partial heterosexual shifts," while 52% experienced, "striking, nearly complete heterosexual shifts" [as measured on the Kinsey Scale] (p. 41).

Later, Birk (1980) discussed subsets of patients whom he treated in group therapy for 2.5-years or longer. These were men who were identified as exclusively homosexual and who had never once experienced heterosexual intercourse. In one subset, 10 out of 14, or 71%, made a "solid heterosexual shift" (p. 387). In terms of *shift*, he made clear that this meant, "…shifts in a person's salient sexual adaptation to life, not total metamorphosis" (p. 387). In other words, they may have continued to have some homosexual feelings, fantasies, and interests. In another subset, 18 out of 29, or 62%, made a "total heterosexual shift" (p. 388), meaning they became absent of any homosexual feelings, fantasies, and interests. Many of those men married.

Finally, group therapy combined with other therapies showed various treatment successes over an 8-year period (Finney, 1960; Buki, 1964; Miller, Bradley, Gross, & Wood, 1968).

5 SEX THERAPIES

Classical sex therapy taught members to overcome fears of
having sex with the opposite sex through various means
including talk/coaching, desensitization, and/or use of
surrogates. Pomeroy (1972) said that Dr. Alfred C. Kinsey,
had records, as early as 1940, "of more than eighty cases of
men who had made a satisfactory heterosexual adjustment
which either accompanied or largely replaced earlier
homosexual experiences" (p. 76). Kinsey, although not
actually a certified sex therapist, was said to have helped
these men by training them to associate with the opposite
sex and "finally starting physical contact of the simplest
kind, working up slowly to intercourse" (p. 76). He did
mention however, that homosexual fantasies were not
always eradicated. According to Pomeroy, Kinsey gave
this advice to one "homosexual boy" who wanted to

change:

> Do not be discouraged if you find the male still
> arousing you more than the female; it may take time
> and abundant heterosexual experience to bring you
> satisfaction equal to what you have know in the
> homosexual. Sometimes, however, I have known
> the homosexual to change almost overnight, as a
> result of a fortunate satisfactory heterosexual
> experience. (p. 77)

Conrad and Wincze (1976) treated 3 male homosexuals with masturbatory conditioning (orgasmic reconditioning); whereas the 3 men were pleased with being able to perform with women and at the same time had no thought or a need for male sexual partners. The men reported to be comfortable performing heterosexual sex after treatment. Thus, the study was considered successful.

Masters and Johnson's (1979) treatment of 90 homosexuals led to many of them being able to perform heterosexually. A 28.4% failure rate was reported after a 6-year follow-up (Schwartz & Masters, 1984). Masters and Johnson chose to report failure rates to avoid vague concepts of "success", but by implication, over 70% of their patients achieved some degree of success toward their self-identified goal of diminishing unwanted homosexuality and developing their heterosexual potential.

6 HYPNOSIS

Hypnosis is known to be helpful as it allows for clarification, extinction of former associations, and formation of new conditional associations. In the case of male homosexuality, the former associations have been said to be too much closeness with mothering coupled with not enough fathering (e.g. in the cases of absent or aloof fathers). Although Charcot and Magnan (1882) held to the theory that homosexuality was congenital, they applied hypnosis to an undisclosed number of said "homosexual men" and reported "success" in that those patients "became heterosexual" (Horstman, 1972, p. 5).

Albert von Schrenck-Notzing (1895), by use of hypnotic suggestion, treated 32 cases of "sexual perversions" (Prince, 1898, p. 237). Twenty of those patients had homosexual desires, behaviors, or both. von Schrenck-Notzing used the term "contrary sexual feeling"

(p. 117), or "contrary sexual instinct" (p. 217) to describe them, which meant they "had impulse toward the same sex with diminution or entire absence of feeling for the opposite sex" (p. 117). Of the 32 cases, 12 cases (37.5%) were said to be "cured" (Prince, 1898, p. 256). *Cured* meant patients were completely able to "combat fixed ideas, deepen a sense of duty, self control, and right mindedness" (p. 255).

Regardie (1949) presented a case of a homosexual identified man who was treated with hypnosis seeking heterosexual adjustment. After hypnosis and other psychotherapy processes, the patient's "social, domestic and social adjustment continu[ed] in a highly satisfactory manner [and] homosexual fantasies no longer occurred, nor did men 'intrigue' him as they passed him on the street" (p. 565).

Alexander (1967) treated a man using hypnosis (trance-states) and non-trance states. The trance states enforced the extinction, while the non-trance sessions, reinforced them. The man was married to a woman, but lacked tenderness and sexual attraction to her. When he did have sex with his wife, he though of other men. After this treatment, "…when having sex relations with his wife he no longer found himself thinking about other men, as he had before treatment, but exclusively about her. He believed his problem solved when, after the last treatment, he found himself entirely free from actual homosexual desires or temptations" (p. 183).

Roper (1967) treated 15 homosexual men from a general psychiatric practice, and out of them, 4 showed *mild improvement* as measured by the Kinsey Scale. During deep trance states, change in sexual orientation was suggested to the patients. He concluded by saying that, "...homosexual behavior can be changed by hypnotherapy if a deep trance level of hypnosis is reached." (p. 327).

Cafiso (1983) reported successfully treating a homosexual man by strengthening his ego through hypnosis, which led to the patient reporting new heterosexual interests and a remission of old homosexual interests.

7 PHARMACOLOGY

Owensby (1940) reported that 6 patients ceased all homosexual behavior due to the use of Metrazol in a follow up of 6 weeks to 18 months. Similar findings with the use of Brevital, in conjunction with Wolpe's relaxation methods, were found in Kraft's (1967) report.

Buki (1964) conducted a clinical trial using tranylcypromine with 36 male patients between the ages of 19 and 34-years-old who had "homosexual traits". After the expiration of the trial time periods (up to 90 days), "the clinical examinations show[ed] an unexpected good control over homosexual activities and impulsions with 13 patients" (p. 306).

Golwyn and Sevlie (1993) reported adventitious change in the sexual orientation of a 23-year-old homosexual male. After receiving Phenelzine for shyness and anxiety, the man reported he no longer had sexual interest in other men. The authors concluded, "Social phobia may be a hidden contributing factor in some instances of homosexual behavior and that Phenelzine, like other dopaminergic agents, might facilitate male heterosexual activity" (p. 40).

A serendipitous finding of fluoxetine-associated suppression of ego-dystonic homosexual activity in a 53-year-old male for a period of thirteen years was reported by Elmore (2002). The patient's determination to remain sexually abstinent was said to be key a successful outcome.

8 MORE EFFORTS

Some outcomes have been documents whereas the specific method or type of modality was vague. Woodward (1958) asserted 28 of the 48 patients who completed forensic treatment no longer reported having homosexual impulses. Seven of them moved to the full heterosexual category on the Kinsey Scale. Whitener and Nikelly (1964) relate that 30 homosexual college students in treatment showed good results in one-third of selected cases. Braaten and Darling (1965) also conducted a study on college students, and found that 29 out of 100 "overt homosexuals" (those who engaged in homosexual behavior), and 21 out of 100 "covert homosexuals" (those not engaged in homosexual behavior, but had impulses, dreams, or fantasies) showed "movement toward heterosexuality as a result of therapy (not implying completely switched from homosexuality)" (p. 293).

Experiential electrode brain stimulation, with the purpose to change sexuality, did not gain popularity past the 1970s, and the literature on the procedures remained scant. Moan and Heath (1972) conducted experiential septal stimulation on a 24-year-old, clinical, fixed, overt homosexual male patient with the purpose to explore the possibility of using it to bring about heterosexual behavior. After completing the procedure's protocol, the patient's mood improved, he was more relaxed, and he became sexually interested in heterosexuality (he began watching heterosexual pornography), and later he participated in sexual intercourse with a female.

Liss and Welner (1973) recounted a client who received supportive therapy after failed attempts with aversion therapy. They reported that there was a complete reversal in his sexual behavior and that he became attracted to women. The authors did not disclose however whether or not the client's homosexual fantasies or attraction to men remained.

The Kinsey Institute writers acknowledged that some homosexual adults have allegedly been "cured" by brain surgery to destroy "inappropriate" sexual response centers (Bell, Weinberg, & Hammersmith, 1981, p. 219).

Cummings (2007) during the 20 years he was at Kaiser-Permanente (1959-1979) in San Francisco, saw over 2,000 patients with same-sex attraction. Of those he saw in psychotherapy, 67% had good outcomes. He did not attempt to reorient same sex attraction to heterosexuality unless the patient strongly indicated this as the therapeutic goal. Twenty percent of the 67% successful psychotherapies did so reorient.

Jones and Yarhouse (2011) conducted replicated and longitudinal research with subjects who completed religious sexual orientation change efforts. Of the 61 subjects, 23% reported success in the form of conversion to heterosexual orientation and functioning. On average, statistically significant decreases in homosexual orientation were reported across the entire sample and the attempt to change orientation was said to *not* lead to increases in psychological distress on average.

9 CONSUMER REPORTS

Nicolosi, Byrd, and Potts (2000), with large efforts from
the *National Association for Research and Therapy of
Homosexuality* (NARTH), retrospectively surveyed 882
dissatisfied homosexuals with a 70-item, client-answered
scale. After receiving therapy or engaging in self-help,
over 34% of the participants said they shifted from an
exclusively homosexual identified orientation to an
exclusively or almost exclusively heterosexual orientation.
Of the 318 who identified as exclusively homosexual
before treatment, 56, or 17.6%, reported that they viewed
themselves as exclusively heterosexual at the time of the
study.

With a smaller sample, Beckstead (2001) used a
structural interview with 18 men and 2 women who
claimed to have benefited from sexual orientation therapy.
He reported that while their sense of peace and contention

improved, he was not convinced of a change in sexual orientation. He stated, "Overall, a change in how to define sexual identity seemed to occur rather than a direct change in sexual orientation" (p. 103).

Shidlo and Schroeder (2002) interviewed (via 90-minute interviews, either in person or by telephone) 182 men and 20 women who were consumers of sexual orientation conversion interventions to find out how they perceived its harmfulness and helpfulness. The researchers recruited participants by advertising on gay and lesbian websites, in e-mail lists and newspapers, in non-gay newspapers, and via direct mailings to gay and ex-gay organizations. Of the 202 participants, 176 were considered as having failed conversion therapy and 26 as having been successful. Twelve were still struggling in that they reported "slips" or some incidences of homosexuality; 6 were not still struggling with same-sex attractions, in that they were managing them; and 8 were termed to be in a "heterosexual shift period" (p. 253), whereas they rated 3 or less on the 7-point Kinsey scale, self-labeled as heterosexual, reported having heterosexual behaviors and in a heterosexual relationship, and denied homosexual behavior.

Spitzer (2003), from Columbia University, interviewed 143 male and 57 female subjects who had participated in sexual reorientation processes by using a telephonic interview consisting of 114 closed-ended questions. Prior to intervention (using the Sexual Attraction Scale, "PRE"), 46% of the males and 42% of the females reported exclusive same-sex attraction. After intervention, (using the Sexual Attraction Scale, "POST") 17% of the males and 54% of the females retrospectively reported exclusive opposite-sex attraction. By way of his findings, Spitzer stated, "Thus, there is evidence that change in sexual orientation following some form of reparative therapy does occur in some gay men and lesbians" (p. 403).

Karten (2006) examined the sexual reorientation efforts of 117 dissatisfied same-sex attracted men who had undergone some type of intervention to change orientation. Using a 7-point sexual self-identity scale with 1 indicating exclusive homosexuality and 7 indicating exclusive heterosexuality, he found that on average at the onset of intervention, men reported a mean score of 4.81 (4-5 = predominantly homosexual with incidental heterosexuality). After intervention, they reported a mean score of 2.57 (2-3 = predominantly heterosexual, or equally heterosexual and homosexual). The shift was statistically significant. The author explained that these participants sought SOCE, not due to societal pressures as so often suggested, but rather due to their own identified intrinsic values (Karten & Wade, 2010).

10 META-ANALYSES and SYNTHESES

Clippinger's (1974) meta-analysis of the collective treatment results of homosexuality demonstrated that out of 785 homosexuals treated from various reports, 307 (40%) made a shift from homosexual to heterosexual.

E. C. James (1978) concluded that when the results of 101 reports from 1929 to 1976 were combined, approximately 35% of homosexual subjects *recovered*, and another 27% *improved*. The combined totals of those recovered or improved totaled 534. Based on this finding, she concluded that pessimistic attitudes about the prognosis for homosexuals changing their sexual orientation are not warranted, saying: "Significant improvement and even complete recovery are entirely possible ..." (p. 183). This language seemed to correlate to earlier, for example, Glover (1960) who defined *recovery* or *cure* to mean that of full extension of heterosexual identity, feelings, impulses, and behaviors, and improved to mean increased ego integration and capacity to control homosexual impulses, to a lesser degree than before treatment.

Jones and Yarhouse (2000) used meta-analysis to review 30 studies conducted between the years of 1954-1994. Of the 327 subjects from all the studies examined, 108, or 33%, of them were reported to have made at least some heterosexual shift.

Byrd and Nicolosi (2002) used the meta-analytic technique for 146 studies evaluating treatment efficacy. Most studies were published prior to 1975, 14 of which were published between 1969 and 1982 and were used for the outcome analysis. The analysis revealed that the treatment for homosexuality was significantly more effective than alternative treatments or control groups for homosexuals. They concluded that the average patient receiving treatment was better off than 79% of those undergoing alternative treatments or when compared to pretreatment scores on several outcome measures.

11 CONCLUSION

This report narrowly focused on reports with clients judged successfully treated. Having that said, it means that just as there are reports showing success, there are ones that show failure. It would be just as easy to produce a report showing treatment failure. As with everything, there are two sides to the coin.

Although there had been variants of treatment modes and attitudes across various disciplines towards the treatment of homosexuality (Lamberd, 1971), much of the premise for therapy aimed at changing sexual orientation had been that the homosexual condition was developmental in nature (hence, psychoanalysis) or learned (hence, cognitive behavioral therapies, sex therapies, and others) and could be changed to some level of heterosexual adjustment, including exclusive heterosexual behavior in some cases. The outcomes of interventions aimed at

changing sexual orientation, to whatever degree, varied.
The outcome measures or *treatment successes* were
generally defined by a shift toward heterosexuality either
through self-reports (case studies), or through various
measurements.

Describing successful outcomes varied, not only by
instrumentation, but also by use of language. For example,
some reporters would use the term *cure* (e.g. Glover, 1960;
van den Cappon, 1965; Aardweg, 1986), while others
would use *recover* or *improve* (e.g. Ellis, 1956, 1965; S.
James, 1978). The latter meaning a lesser degree than the
former. Still others used various degrees thereof (e.g.
Schmidt, Castell, & Brown, 1965; Roper, 1967). E.C.
James (1978) based on her findings concluded:
"Significant improvement and even complete recovery
[were] entirely possible ..." (p. 183). This language
("complete cure") seemed to correlate to earlier, for
example, Glover (1960) who defined *cure* to mean that of
full extension of heterosexual identity, feelings, impulses,
and behaviors, and *improved* to mean increased ego
integration and capacity to control homosexual impulses, to
a lesser degree than before treatment. Given these
definitions, *recover* and *cure* appear synonymous and

static. While other forms described such as *improve* or *shift* appeared as synonymous, but not as static.

Various paradigms and approaches have been used, as discussed. Psychoanalysis has been applied, with said success, by helping patients resolve Oedipal conflicts. Group work seemed to claim success in helping patients reveal sexual practices, accomplish competition with members, see reactions to opposite sex, feel part of the group, and work through transferences. Aversion therapy was accomplished by the association of an unpleasant subjective experience with the attractive stimulus that it was required to make unattractive. Chemical methods (apomorphine) or electronic stimulation had been used to create the unpleasant and anxiety-producing stimulus. Classical sex therapy taught members to overcome fears of having sex with the opposite sex through various means including talk/coaching, desensitization, and/or use of surrogates. Combining therapies, and other methods also claimed success.

The main problem with reports was in thoroughly defining terms, specifically *sexual orientation, homosexuality,* and *heterosexuality,* and what change or success meant in the long run. The methodology and techniques within the reports varied. Since there was no consensus of what a successful outcome was, each study

maintained independent claims for defining it. However, in

reference to outcomes, according to Kirkpatrick and

Morgan (1980):

> Heterosexual desires may emerge and may lead to heterosexual relationships as the preferred source of satisfaction [however]...good and responsible therapy is not defined by this outcomes but by relief of distress and increase in personal options for pleasure and for enhancing the quality of life. (p. 374)

They go on to say,

> A patient's intent to change object preference as a therapeutic goal may fluctuate considerably during treatment. As therapy proceeds and anxieties are appropriately reduced, and internal conflicts are separated from contemporary relationships, heterosexuality may become more gratifying or may begin to offer a more fulfilling life. On the other hand, as the impact of social disapproval is lessened through an increase of inner strength and self-esteem, homosexuality may become less guilt producing and a more satisfying homosexuality may become available. (p. 369)

Kirkpatrick and Morgan (1980) say the only

invariable goal in therapeutic work is the "increased

understanding on the patient's part and an increased

capacity for her to use her mind" (p. 369).

Marmor (1980) observed that it was not always clear whether patients in treatment were exclusively homosexual or if they were a 3, 4, or 5 on the Kinsey scale, for example. Further, he pointed out that to say a patient benefited from therapy may not necessarily mean a total abandonment of homosexual object-choice had been achieved. He said,

> A group 5 or group 6 may be enabled to shift to a group 3 or group 4 pattern, or may be helped toward a more stable and satisfying life in general – certainly positive therapeutic results – yet they should not be put in the same category as a total shift in object-preference. (p. 277)

The prognosis for treatment success seemed to be conditional. For example, while Ovesey, Gaylin and Haydin (1963) reported 3 successful treated male homosexuals, treatment success was said to be more favorable, for example, with men who had strong motivations, strong ego-strength, greater heterosexual social identification, and who were masculine sexually identified, among other factors (Ovesey & Gaylin, 1963). Marmor (1980) seemed to agree that certain factors contributed to outcomes that were more favorable. These included younger patients, patients who had previous heterosexual experience, those who had a later onset of the homosexual experience, and those with stronger gender identification.

Treatments seemed to follow some sort of fundamental assumption about homosexuality. Psychoanalysts for example, reporting successful treatment of homosexuality tended to share three fundamental assumptions: 1) that homosexuality was pathologic and not based on a constitutional, biological basis, 2) that the homosexual act was an overdetermined symptom with specific unconscious meaning, and 3) that homosexuality was treatable and normal heterosexual direction and drive could be established.

In terms of the theory, or believe system driving therapy, Feldman (1956) felt that human beings were biologically heterosexual and that the therapists' "real goal was to bring the patient to their biological given heterosexual relationship" (p. 93). This was drawn on the believe system that "man is born for woman and woman is born for man. Anything outside this picture means only that, once upon a time, a trouble arose which diverted the individual from his normal path of life" (p. 94)

These outcome studies, like all studies, had limitations. Particularly, the single case studies had limits because the data was objective, based on an individual therapist's reports, and not generalized to a larger body. Anecdotal accounts are just that, and are not well received when more scientific means of study are available. While some studies rely on larger samples, they are often limited by self-reported data, non-randomization, retrospective issues, and other issues such as cognitive dissonance and social desirability. Many studies are limited due to the absence of control groups and correlative values, while many studies are criticized for lacking ideal measuring techniques, having methodological flaws, and inadequate longitudinal and replicative factors.

A behavoralist himself, who has reported successful interventions aimed at changing homosexuality, Birk (1980) criticized behavioral techniques and premises generally used to treat homosexual behavior. For one, he claimed there had been a lack of emphasis on oedipal based fears. Additionally, he said that the use of aversion was overemphasized to the degree of "paralytic shortcoming" (p. 379). Birk (1974) also noted that conditioning technique was inferior when absent of intensive long-term group therapy, as recorded in samples whose Kinsey's ratings were less improved 1-year *after* conditioning. This meant that during the conditioning period, they showed very successful progress, but sometime afterwards, they relapsed. This was largely due to the technique, in absence of intensive therapy, rather than the patient's actual potential.

Others felt the therapeutic process was not as important as was the patient's determination. Marmor (1980) asserted that,

> ...giving up a behavioral pattern that is a major, if not the main, source of a person's erotic satisfaction is understandably enormous, and the fact that somewhere between 25 and 50 percent of homosexuals who seek to change their main sexual orientation are able to do so is more a tribute to the strength of their motivation than it is to the specific therapeutic approach involved. (p. 277)

Consumer survey studies (e.g. Spitzer, 2003) have been criticized as some of the respondents came from religious-based interventions and therefore judged to not be therapeutic or valid in the scientific realm. Critics judged participant's changes to be due to religious convictions and not scientific interventions. The mental health arena has, however, given some recognition to religious-mediated interventions in the past. For example, the *American Journal of Psychiatry* published a study by Pattison and Pattison (1980) who reported successful religiously mediated change of 11 homosexual men while they participated in a Pentecostal fellowship program. They used both pre and post surveys. On the post-change survey, 5 of the 11 participants reported no homosexual fantasies, behaviors, or impulses (0 on the Kinsey Scale). Three men reported a Kinsey rating of 1, and 3 other men reported a rating of 2.

Studies have additionally been weakened because *sexual orientation* is generally not clearly defined or understood (Gonsoriek, Sell, & Weinrich, 1995; Sell, 1997). For example, one may define himself or herself as *heterosexual*, yet still have homosexual behaviors or tendencies; while another person may define himself or herself as *heterosexual* and have no homosexual tendencies. Yet, both describe themselves as *heterosexual*. As for reporting success rates, complications remain. For example, in some reports, clinicians stated *success* in that a client had heterosexually married, however being married does not mean one is necessarily exclusively heterosexual.

The literature does not support homosexuality as a fixed state. For example, in the study of men by Kinsey, Pomeroy, & Martin (1948), while they found 10% of the sample admitting to homosexual incidence during some point in their lifetime, only 4% were exclusively homosexual throughout their lives. Some scholars assert that sexuality is fluid (Bell & Weinberg, 1978; Weinrich &

Klein, 2002; Kernberg, 2002). According to Schneider, Brown, and Glassgold (2002), *sexual orientation* is perplexing because one's self-identified sexual orientation may not be congruent with his or her sexual behavior. They say sexual orientation is best conceptualized as a continuum, rather than categorical.

Treatment aimed at changing sexual orientation has become political (Zucker, 2003) and embedded in a culture war (Drescher, 2003). Some feel that there is nothing to change except society's views about homosexuality (Halpert, 2000). Some feel treatment directed at changing sexual orientation only fosters a shameful attitude toward homosexuals, whom are no longer classified as mentally ill (Green, 2003). Critics of these specific therapies claimed they can be harmful, while anecdotal accounts said the same (Duberman, 1991; Shidlo, Schroeder & Drescher, 2001; Shidlo & Schroeder, 2002). All the while agreeing, Forstein (2001) said, "There are no studies … to provide [this]" (p. 177).

Largely, the shift of the treatment of homosexuality, due to its removal from diagnostic criteria as a mental illness, has largely evolved from amelioration to acceptance and normalization. The topic of sexual conversion remains an ongoing social debate within various medias. The

American Psychological Association (APA) has warned against the use of therapies aimed at changing sexual orientation (American Psychological Association, 1997, 2009). They warn that users of reparative therapies take an *a priori* assumption that homosexuals are sick and need cure. They appointed a task force who generated a report that addressed many issues, particularly education, training, and research as it pertained to therapeutic interventions (American Psychological Association, 2009).

A strong argument exists to hold a place at the clinical table for those who seek change or shifts in their sexual orientation (Byrd, 2003; Rosik, 2003). Is it ethical to deny the call for such help, if such help is autonomous to the client and not externally driven (e.g. legal system, social, family, etc)? There is evidence of such calls for help because those who have received assistance and those seeking assistance have collectively stood up to be counted, as once did their openly gay counterparts in the 1970's. On May 22, 1994, in Philadelphia, for the first time in history, the American Psychiatric Association was protested against, not by pro-gay activists, but by a group of people claiming that they had been cured, desired treatment, and that cure was possible for others (Davis, 1994). This was repeated at their 2000 convention in Chicago (Gorner,

2000), and again at the 2006 American Psychological Association Convention in New Orleans (Foust, 2006). But despite this, some states within the United States have passed legislation to prohibit the use of SOCE for minors (Karlamangla, 2013).

The point has been made that there are patients who seek treatment and treatments should be made available (Socarides, et al, 1997; Nicolosi, 2003). The argument is that the APA should not recommend against treatment for unwanted homosexuality as long as there are patients seeking it and therapists willing to provide the service. It would simply go against their own ethical standards to deny such treatment, which says that, "Mental health organizations call on their members to respect a person's [client's] right to self-determination" (The American Psychological Association, 2008, p. 3). Certainly, client self-determination is one of the cornerstones of any form of psychological care, and any attempt to ban psychological care for those who have a persistent and marked distress with their homosexual attractions would be a direct violation of the APA's own ethical standards. On the same token, one not distressed with their sexual orientation should not be otherwise directed to change. As Rosik (2003) has asserted, "It is hoped that the viewpoints of both proponents as well as opponents of reorientation treatment will be regarded as having something important to contribute" (p. 28) to the clinical table. Like a coin, two sides remain.

Finally, claiming that homosexuality, *per se*, is not an official mental disorder according to the DSM, is not necessary a prohibition to treat, considering distress and dissatisfaction is always a determinate factor in treating, and is still consistent with the current nature of the DSM and psychotherapy itself. While, it may be problematic to take an *a priori* assumption that homosexuality is a condition ameliorable as the APA and others claim, the same is true for taking an *a priori* assumption that homosexuality is inborn, and not ameliorable given there are those who seek, and have received, such amelioration, and in absence of conclusive evidence of homosexual etiology. As with any therapy, informed consent must be made, and the patient made aware of any possible risks/side effects and benefits.

Reviewing history, homosexuality was officially defined as a mental disorder by the American Psychiatric Association from 1952 to 1973, but has not officially been since then. Following controversy and protests from gay activists at the American Psychiatric Association annual

conferences from 1970 to 1973, the seventh printing of the
Diagnostic and Statistical Manual II (DSM-II) in 1974 no
longer listed homosexuality as a category of disorder. After
talks led by the Dr. Robert Spitzer, who had been involved
in the DSM-II development committee, a vote by the APA
trustees in 1973, confirmed by the wider APA membership
in 1974, had replaced the diagnosis with a milder category
of *sexual orientation disturbance*. If mental illness was
really an illness in the same sense that physical illnesses
were illnesses, the idea of deleting homosexuality or
anything else from the categories of illness by having a
vote would be as absurd as a group of physicians voting to
delete cancer or measles from the concept of disease. But
mental illness *is not* an illness like any other illness. Unlike
physical disease where there are physical facts, or blood
test to confirm, *mental illness* is entirely a question of
values. After homosexuals and advocates protested and
successfully demanded at least a small measure of social
acceptance, it was no longer called a mental illness, or a
disorder (Stevens, 1999).

Nevertheless, considering there were individuals who
were homosexually oriented, yet unsatisfied this way, the
American Psychiatric Association replaced the diagnosis
with the category of *sexual orientation disturbance*. This

was later replaced with the diagnosis of *ego-dystonic homosexuality* in the DSM-III in 1980, but that was removed in 1987 with the release of the DSM-III-R. A category of *sexual disorder not otherwise specified* continued in the DSM-IV, which included "persistent and marked distress about one's sexual orientation" (p. 582).

To date, this is the most comprehensive compilation of studies documenting the outcomes of interventions aimed at changing sexual orientation. Earlier reviews have also concluded that there are reports that have shown to be successful in modify sexual orientation, to varying degrees (e.g. E. C. James, 1978; Throckmorton, 1998). The main limit of this report, however, is that while it presented a bibliographic review of the literature, it did not provide much in the way of a specific in-depth discussion of the studies' weaknesses and strengths. In short however, reporting has been absent of rigorous research methods. Basically, this has been the basis of organizational dismissal of these therapies (e.g. American Psychiatric Association's' Position Statement on Psychological Treatment and Sexual Orientation (American Psychological Association, 1999). However, the point has been made, which asserts, that this statement is unfair. For example, In Spitzer's (2003) study, he said that while the American

Psychiatric Association stated that therapies aimed to change sexual orientation have no "scientific evidence supporting...efficacy" (p. 2), he made the point that such comment could be made for other widely used types of psychotherapy, including Gay Affirmative Therapy (GAT). While the American Psychiatric Association may support GAT, it too has not been subjected to a rigorous study to evidence scientific efficacy.

Overall, the research literature is limited by sampling, assessment, and follow-up issues, however despite the methodological limitations of individual studies, there is nevertheless compelling body of evidence that some individuals can shift identity and/or behavioral components of their sexual orientation after undergoing some type of intervention, or none at all. Most of the research has been conducted on men, however a number of theorists have argued that women's sexuality is more fluid and situationally influenced than men's sexuality. Which begs the question of whether or not therapies aimed at changing sexual orientation would yield results that are more desirable with women.

A gold standard study on interventions to change sexual orientation, like anything studied, would include a randomized design, where some participants receive the treatment and others do not. Ideally, the participants in such a study would not be highly pre-selected (e.g. from certain religious domains) as have been criticized in the past. The ideal study on this topic would assess participants' sexual orientation, before treatment, in multiple ways (e.g., it would assess sexual identity, sexual behavior, sexual fantasies and desires, and physiological sexual arousal to stimuli). After treatment, sexual orientation would continue to be assessed in multiple ways. In addition, ideally, there would be long-term, as well as periodical follow up. In the case of very partisan treatment approaches, such as religious-based therapy and reparative therapy, it would be desirable if those who assessed sexual orientation and who conducted the evaluation study were independent of the partisan agents who were conducting the treatment. Further studies to include qualitative data are needed to broaden the scope about the outcomes of interventions aimed at changing sexual orientation.

Finally, defining and measuring "sexual orientation," reveals significant challenges such as a lack of consensus, narrow interpretations, and lack of construct validity. Researchers who have attempted to measure sexual orientation and its presumed components typically have relied on only a few instruments which have been criticized as inconclusive, oversimplified, loose, and imprecise. Considering the emerging trend to improve research, human rights, and health care delivery to sexual minorities, it is strongly recommended that a comprehensive, multi-component approach to measure sexual orientation be developed and used in future research (Phelan, 2013).

ALPHABETICAL BIBLIOGRAPHY

Alexander, L. (1967). Psychotherapy of sexual deviations with the aid of hypnosis. *American Journal of Clinical Hypnosis, 9*(3), 181-183.

Allen, C. (1952). On the cure of homosexuality II. *International Journal of Sexology, 5,* 139-141.

Allen, C. (1956). The treatment of homosexuality. *Medical Press, 235,* 441-450.

Allen, C. (1958). *Homosexuality: Its nature, causation and treatment.* London: Staples Press.

American Psychiatric Association (1999). Position statement on psychiatric treatment and sexual orientation. *American Journal of Psychiatry, 156,* 1131.

American Psychological Association. (1997). Resolutions *related to lesbian, gay and bisexual issues.* Washington, DC: Author. Retrieved from http://www.apa.org/pi/reslgbc.html

American Psychological Association. (2008). *Answers to your questions: For a better understanding of sexual orientation and homosexuality.* Washington, DC: Author. Retrieved from www.apa.org/topics/sorientation.pdf

American Psychological Association (APA) Task Force on Appropriate Therapeutic Responses to Sexual Orientation. (2009). *Report of the Task Force on*

Appropriate Therapeutic Responses to Sexual Orientation. Washington, DC: Author.

Bancroft, J. H. (1969). Aversion therapy of homosexuality: A pilot study of 10 cases. *British Journal of Psychiatry, 115*, 1417-1431.

Bancroft, J. H. (1970). A comparative study of aversion and desensitization in the treatment of homosexuality. In L. E. Burns & J. L. Worsley (Eds.), *Behavior therapy in the 1970's: A collection of original papers* (pp. 34-56). Oxford, England: John Wright & Sons.

Barlow, D. H. (1973). Increasing heterosexual responsiveness in the treatment of sexual deviation: A review of the clinical and experimental evidence. *Behavior Therapy, 4*, 655-671.

Barlow, D. H., & Agras, W. S. (1973). Fading to increase heterosexual responsiveness in homosexuals. *Journal of Applied Behavior Analysis, 6*, 355-366.

Barlow, D. H., & Durand, V. M. (1995). *Abnormal psychology: An integrative approach*. New York: Brooks/Cole Publishing Company.

Beckstead, A. L. (2001). Cure verses choices: Agendas in sexual reorientation therapy. In A. Shidlo, M. Schroeder, & J. Drescher (Eds.), *Sexual conversion therapy: Ethical, clinical, and research perspectives* (pp. 87-115). Binghamton, NY: Haworth Press.

Bell, A. P., & Weinberg, M. S. (1978). *Homosexualities: A study of diversity among men and women*. New York: Simon & Schuster.

Bell, A. P., Weinberg, M. S., & Hammersmith, S. A. (1981). *Sexual preference*. Bloomington, IN: Indiana University Press.

Berg, C., & Allen, C. (1958). *The problem of homosexuality*. New York: Citadel Press.

Berger, J. (1994). The psychotherapeutic treatment of male homosexuality. *American Journal of Psychotherapy, 48*, 251-261.

Bergin, A. E. (1969). A self-regulation technique for impulse control disorders. *Psychotherapy: Theory, Research and Practice, 6*, 113-118.

Bergler, E. (1956). *Homosexuality: Disease or way of life?* New York: Collier Books.

Beukenkamp, C. (1960). Phantom patricide. *Archives of General Psychiatry, 3*, 282-288.

Bieber, I. (1967). Sexual Deviations II: Homosexuality. In A. M. Freedman, & H. I. Kaplan (Eds.), *Comprehensive textbook of psychiatry* (pp. 963-976). Baltimore: Williams and Wilkins.

Bieber, I., & Bieber, T. B. (1979). Male homosexuality. *Canadian Journal of Psychiatry, 24*, 409-419.

Bieber, I., Dain, H., Dince, P., Drellich, M., Grand, H., Grundlach, R., Kremer, M. W., Rifkin, A. H., Wilbur, C. B., & Bieber, T. B. (1962). *Homosexuality: A psychoanalytic study*. New York: Basic Books.

Bieber, T. B. (1971). Group therapy with homosexuals. In H. I. Kaplan & B. J. Sadock (Eds.), *Comprehensive group psychotherapy* (pp. 518-533). Baltimore: Williams and Wilkins.

Birk, L. (1974). Group psychotherapy for men who are homosexual. *Journal of Sex and Marital Therapy, 1*, 29-52.

Birk, L. (1980). The myth of classical homosexuality: Views of a behavioral psychotherapist. In J. Marmor (Ed.), *Homosexual Behavior* (pp. 376-390). New York: Basic Books.

Birk, L., Miller, E., & Cohler, B. (1970). Group psychotherapy for homosexual men. *Acta Psychiatrica Scandinavica, 218*, 1-33.

Blitch, J., & Haynes, S. (1972). Multiple behavioral techniques in a case of female homosexuality. *Journal of Behavioral Therapy & Experimental Psychiatry, 3*, 319-322.

Braaten, L. J., & Darling, C. D. (1965). Overt and covert homosexual problems among male college students. *Genetic Psychology Monographs, 71*, 269-310.

Buki, R. A. (1964). A treatment program for homosexuals. *Diseases of the Nervous System, 25*(5), 304-307.

Byrd, A.D. (2003). The malleability of homosexuality: A debate long overdue. *Archives of Sexual Behavior, 32*(5), 423-425.

Byrd, A. D., & Nicolosi, J. (2002). A meta-analytic review of treatment of homosexuality. *Psychological Reports, 90*, 1139-1152.

Cafiso, R. (1983). The homosexual: The advantages of hypnotherapy as treatment. *Rivista: International Journal of Psychological Hypnosis, 24*(1), 49-55.

Callahan, E. J., Krumboltz, J. D., & Thoresen, C. E. (Eds.). (1976). *Counseling methods*. New York: Holt, Rinehart, and Winston.

Cantón-Dutari, A. (1974). Combined intervention for controlling unwanted sexual behavior. *Archives of Sexual Behavior, 3*(4), 367-371.

Cantón-Dutari, A. (1976). Combined intervention for controlling unwanted sexual behavior: An extended follow-up. *Archives of Sexual Behavior, 5*(4), 323-325.

Cappon, D. (1965). *Toward an understanding of homosexuality*. Englewood Cliffs, NJ: Prentice-Hall, Inc.

Caprio, F. S. (1954). *Female homosexuality: A psychodynamic study of lesbianism*. New York: Citadel Press.

Cautela, J. R. (1967). Covert sensitization. *Psychological Reports, 20*, 459-468.

Cautela, J. R. & Kasterbaum, R. (1967). A reinforcement survey schedule for the use in therapy, training, and research. *Psychological Reports, 20*, 1115-1130.

Cautela, J., & Wisocki, P. (1971). Covert sensitization for the treatment of sexual deviations. *Psychological Record, 21*, 37-48.

Charcot, J., & Magnan, M (1882). Inversion of the genital sense. *Archives de Neurology, 7*, 12.

Clippinger, J. A. (1974). Homosexuality can be cured. *Corrective and Social Psychiatry and Journal of Behavioral Technology, Methods, and Therapy, 20*(2), 15-28.

Coates, S. (1962). Homosexuality and the Rorschach test. *The British Journal of Medical Psychology, 35*, 177-190.

Conrad, S. R., & Wincze, J. P. (1976). Orgasmic reconditioning: A controlled study of its effects upon sexual arousal and behavior of adult male homosexuals. *Behavior Therapy, 7*, 155-166.

Cummings, N. (2007). Former APA President Dr. Nicholas Cummings describes his work with SSA clients. Retrieved April 2, 2007, from http://www.narth.com/docs/cummings.html

Curran, D., & Parr, D. (1957). Homosexuality: An analysis of 100 male cases seen in private practice. *British Medical Journal, 112*, 797-801.

Davis, M. (1994, May 22). Protesters blast APA's position. *The Philadelphia Inquirer*, p. B4.

Davison G. C., & Wilson, G. T. (1973). Attitudes of behavior therapists towards homosexuality. *Behavior Therapy, 45*(5), 686-696.

Drescher, J. (2003). The Spitzer study and the culture wars. *Archives of Sexual Behavior, 32*(5), 431-432.

Drescher, J., Stein, T. S., & Byne, W. M. (2005). Homosexuality, gay and lesbian identities, and homosexual behavior. In B. J. Sadock, & V. A. Sadock (Eds.), *Comprehensive textbook of psychiatry* (pp. 1936-1969). Baltimore: Lippincott Williams and Wilkins.

Duberman, M. (1991*). Cures: A gay man's odyssey.* New York: E P Dutton.

Eidelberg, L. (1956). Analysis of a case of a male homosexual. In S. Lorand & M. Balint (Eds.), *Perversions: Psychodynamics and therapy* (pp. 279-289). New York: Gramery Books.

Eliasberg, W. G. (1954). Group treatment of homosexuals on probation. *Group Psychotherapy, 7,* 218-226.

Ellis, A. (1952). On the cure of homosexuality. *International Journal of Sexology, 5,* 148-150.

Ellis, A. (1956). The effectiveness of psychotherapy with individuals who have severe homosexual problems. *Journal of Consulting Psychology, 20*(3), 191.

Ellis, A. (1959). A homosexual treated with rational therapy. *Journal of Clinical Psychology, 15*(3), 338-343.

Ellis, A. (1965). *Homosexuality: Its causes and cure.* New York: Lyle Stuart, Inc.

Elmore, J. L. (2002). Fluoxetine-Associated remission of ego-dystonic male homosexuality. *Sexuality and Disability, 20*(2), 149-151.

Feldman, M. P., & MacCulloch, M. J. (1964). A systematic approach to the treatment of homosexuality by conditioned aversion: A preliminary report. *The American Journal of Psychiatry, 121*, 167-171.

Feldman, M. P., & MacCulloch, M. J. (1965). The application of anticipatory avoidance learning to the treatment of homosexuality: Theory, techniques and preliminary results. *Behavior Research and Therapy, 3*, 165-183.

Feldman, M. P., & MacCulloch, M. J. (Eds.). (1971). *Homosexual behavior: Therapy and assessment.* New York: Pergamon Press.

Feldman, M. P., MacCulloch, M. J., Mellor, V., & Pinschof, J. M. (1966). The sexual orientation method. *Behaviour Research and Therapy, 4*, 289-300.

Feldman, M. P., MacCulloch, M. J., & Orford, J. F. (1971). Conclusions and speculations. In M. P. Feldman, & M. J. MacCulloch (Eds.), *Homosexual behavior: Therapy and assessment* (pp. 156-188). New York: Pergamon Press.

Feldman, S. S. (1956). On homosexuality. In S. Lorand & M. Balint (Eds.), *Perversions: Psychodynamics and therapy* (pp. 71-97). New York: Gramery Books.

Finney, J. C. (1960). Homosexuality treated by combined psychotherapy. *Journal of Social Therapy, 6*(1), 27-34.

Fookes, B. H. (1969). Some experiences in the use of aversion therapy in male homosexuality, exhibitionism, and fetishism-transvestism. *British Journal of Psychiatry, 115*, 339-341.

Forstein, M. (2001). Overview of ethical and research issues in sexual orientation therapy. In Ariel Shidlo, Michael Schroeder, & Jack Drescher (Eds.), *Sexual Conversion therapy: ethical, clinical and research perspectives* (pp. 167-179). Binghamton, NY: Haworth Press.

Foust, M. (2006, August 14). Ex-homosexuals protest APA's position on homosexuality. *BP News*. Retrieved December. 9, 2006, from http://www.sbcbaptistpress.org/bpnews.asp?ID=23786

Frankl, V. E. (1967). *Psychotherapy and Existentialism*. Harmondsworth: Penguin.

Freeman, W. M., & Meyer, R. G. (1975). A behavioral alteration of sexual preferences in the human male. *Behavior Therapy, 6*, 206-212.

Freud, A. (1968, original 1952). Studies in passivity (1952 [1949-1951]): Part 1 Notes on homosexuality. In *The writings of Anna Freud Volume IV: Indications for child analysis and other papers* (pp. 245-256). New York: International Universities Press.

Freud, S. (1920a). Beyond the pleasure principle. In J. Strachey (Ed.), *Standard Edition, Vol 18* (pp. 1-64). London: Hogarth Press.

Freud, S. (1920b). The psychogenesis of a case of homosexuality in a woman. In J. Strachey (Ed.), *Standard Edition, Vol 18* (pp 145-172). London: Hogarth Press.

Freud, S. (1951). A letter from Freud. *American Journal of Psychiatry, 107*, 786-787.

Freund, K. (1960). Some problems in the treatment of homosexuality. In H. J. Eysenck, (Ed.), *Behaviour therapy and the neuroses* (pp. 312-326). London: Pergamon Press.

Freund, K. (1967). Diagnosing homo- or heterosexuality and erotic age-preference by means of a psychophysiological test. *Behavoiral research and Therapy, 5*, 209-228.

Glover, E. (1960). *The roots of crime: Selected papers in psychoanalysis, Vol 2*. New York: International Universities Press.

Golwyn, D. H., & Sevlie, C. P. (1993). Adventitious change in homosexual treatment of social phobia with Phenelzine. *Journal of Clinical Psychiatry, 54*(1), 39-40.

Gonsoriek, J. C., Sell, R. L., & Weinrich, J. D. (1995). Definition and measurement of sexual orientation. *Suicide and Life Threatening Behavior, 25*(Suppl.), 40-51.

Gordon, A. (1930). The history of a homosexual: His difficulties and triumphs. *Medical Journal and Record, 131*, 152-156.

Gorner, P. (2000, May 18) Analysts drop gay therapy discussion reorientation efforts off meeting agenda. *Chicago Tribune*, p. A1.

Gray, J. (1970). Case conference: Behavior therapy in a patient with homosexual fantasies and heterosexual anxiety. *Journal of Behavioral Therapy & Experimental Psychiatry, 1*, 225-232.

Green, R. J. (2003). When therapists do not want their clients to be homosexual: A response to Rosik's article. *Journal of Marital and Family Therapy, 29*, 29-38.

Greenspoon, J., & Lamal, P. (1987). A behavioristic approach. In L. Diamant (Ed.), *Male and female homosexuality: Psychological approaches* (pp. 109-127). New York: Hemisphere Publishing Corp.

Hadden, S. B. (1957). Attitudes towards and approaches to the problem of homosexuality. *Pennsylvania Medical Journal, 60*, 1195-1198.

Hadden, S. B. (1958). Treatment of homosexuality by individual and group psychotherapy. *American Journal of Psychiatry, 114*, 810-815.

Hadden, S. B. (1966). Treatment of male homosexuals in groups. *International Journal of Group Psychotherapy, 16*(1), 13-22.

Hadden, S. B. (1971). Group therapy for homosexuals. *Medical Aspects of Human Sexuality, 5*(1), 116-127.

Hadfield, J. A. (1958). The cure of homosexuality. *British Medical Journal, 1*(2), 1323-1326.

Hadfield, J. A. (1966). Origins of homosexuality. *British Medical Journal, 7,* 678.

Haldeman, D. (1994). The practice and ethics of sexual orientation conversion therapy. *Journal of Consulting and Clinical Psychology, 62*(2), 221-227.

Hallam, R. S., & Rachman, S. (1972). Some effects of aversion therapy on patients with sexual disorders. *Behaviour Research and Therapy, 10*(2), 171-180.

Halpert, S. C. (2000). 'If it aint broke, don't fix it': Ethical considerations regarding conversion therapies. *International Journal of Sexuality and Gender Studies, 5*(1), 19-35.

Hanson, R., & Adesso, V. (1972). A multiple behavioral approach to male homosexual behavior: A case study. *Journal of Behavioral Therapy & Experimental Psychiatry, 3,* 323-325.

Hatterer, L. (1970). *Changing homosexuality in the male.* New York: McGraw Hill Book Co.

Herman, S. H., Barlow, D. H., & Agras, W. S. (1974). An experimental analysis of classical conditioning as a method of increasing heterosexual arousal in homosexuals. *Behavior Therapy, 5,* 33-47.

Horstman, W. R. (1972). *Homosexuality and psychopathology: A study of the MMPI responses of homosexual and heterosexual male college students.* Unpublished doctoral dissertation, University of Oregon, Eugene.

Huff, F. (1970). The desensitization of a homosexual. *Behavioral Research Therapy, 8,* 99-102.

Jacobi, J. (1969). Case of homosexuality. *Journal of Analytical Psychology, 14,* 48-64.

James, B. (1962). Case of a homosexual treated by aversion therapy. *British Medical Journal, 5280,* 768-770.

James B. & Early, D. F. (1963). Aversion Therapy for Homosexuality. *British Medical Journal, 1*(5329), 538-550.

James, E. C. (1978). *Treatment of homosexuality: A reanalysis and synthesis of outcome studies.* Unpublished doctoral dissertation, Brigham Young University, Provo, Utah.

James, S. (1978). Treatment of homosexuality II. Superiority of desensitization/arousal as compared with anticipatory avoidance conditioning: Results of a controlled trial. *Behavioral Therapy, 9,* 28-36.

Jones, S. L., & Yarhouse, M. A. (2000). *Homosexuality: The use of scientific research in the church's moral debate.* Downers Grove, IL: InterVarsity Press.

Jones, S. L., & Yarhouse, M. A. (2011). A longitudinal study of attempted religiously mediated sexual orientation change. *Journal of Sex and Martial Therapy, 37*, 404–427.

Karlamangla, S. (2013, November 10). New Jersey court ruling another blow to gay conversion therapies. *Los Angeles Times*. Retrieved from http://articles.latimes.com/2013/nov/10/nation/la-na-nn-gay-conversion-new-jersey-ban-20131109

Karten, E. (2006). *Sexual reorientation efforts in dissatisfied same-sex attracted men: What does it really take to change*. Unpublished doctoral dissertation, Fordham University, New York, NY.

Karten, E. L., & Wade, J. C. (2010). Sexual orientation change efforts in men: A client perspective. *Journal of Men's Studies, 18*, 84–102.

Kaye, H. E., Berl, S., Clare, J., Eleston, M. R., Gershwin, B. S., Gershwin, P., Kogan, L.S., Torda, C., & Wilbur, B. (1967). Homosexuality in women. *Archives of General Psychiatry, 17*, 626-634.

Kendrick, S., & McCullough, J. (1972). Sequential phases of covert reinforcement and covert sensitization in the treatment of homosexuality. *Journal of Behavioral Therapy & Experimental Psychiatry, 3*, 229-231.

Kernberg, O. F. (2002). Unresolved issues in the psychoanalytic theory of homosexuality and bisexuality. *Journal of Gay & Lesbian Psychotherapy, 6*(1), 9-27.

Kinsey, A. C., Pomeroy, W. B., & Martin, C. E. (1948). *Sexual behavior in the human male*. Philadelphia: W.B. Saunders.

Kirkpatrick, M., & Morgan, C. (1980). Psychodynamic psychotherapy of female homosexuality. In J. Marmor (Ed.) *Homosexual behavior: A modern reappraisal* (pp. 357-375). New York: Basic Books.

Klein, F. (1978). *The bisexual option.* New York: Arbor House.

Kraft, T. (1967). A case of homosexuality treated by systematic desensitization. *American Journal of Psychotherapy, 21*(4), 815-821.

Kraft, T. (1970). Systematic desensitization in the treatment of homosexuality. *Behavior Research and Therapy, 8,* 319.

Larson, D. (1970). An adaptation of the Feldman and MacCulloch approach to treatment of homosexuality by the application of anticipatory avoidance learning. *Behavioral Research and Therapy, 8,* 209-210.

Lamberd, W. G. (1969). The treatment of homosexuality as a monosymptomatic phobia. *The American Journal of Psychiatry, 126,* 512-518.

Lamberd, W. G. (1971). Viewpoints: What outcome can be expected in psychotherapy? *Medical Aspects of Human Sexuality, 5*(12), 90-105.

Liss, J. L., & Welner, A. (1973). Change in homosexual orientation. *American Journal of Psychotherapy, 27*(1), 102-104.

Litman, R. E. (1961). Psychotherapy of a homosexual man in heterosexual group. *International Journal of Group Psychotherapy, 11*(4), 440-448.

London, L. S., & Caprio, F. S. (1950). *Sexual deviations: A Psychodynamic approach.* Washington, DC: Linacre Press, Inc.

Lorand, S. (1956). The therapy of perversions. In S. Lorand & M. Balint (Eds.), *Perversions: Psychodynamics and therapy* (pp. 290-307). New York: Gramery Books.

MacCulloch, M. J., & Feldman, M. P. (1967). Aversion therapy in management of 43 homosexuals. *British Medical Journal, 2*, 594-597.

MacIntosh, H. (1994). Attitudes and experiences of psychoanalysis in analyzing homosexual patients. *Journal of the American Psychoanalytic Association, 42*, 1183-1207.

Maletzky, B. M., & George, F. S. (1973). The treatment of homosexuality by "assisted" covert sensitization. *Journal of Behavior Research and Therapy, 11*(4), 655-657.

Mandel, K. (1970). Preliminary report of a new aversion therapy for male homosexuals. *Behavioral Research & Therapy, 8*, 93-95.

Marmor, J. (1980). *Homosexual behavior.* New York: Basic Books.

Marquis, J. (1970). Orgasmic reconditioning: Changing sexual object choice through controlling masturbation fantasies. *Journal of Behavioral Therapy & Experimental Psychiatry, 1,* 263-271.

Masters, W., & Johnson, V. (1979). *Homosexuality in perspective.* Boston: Little, Brown.

Mather, N. J. (1966). The treatment of homosexuality by aversion therapy. *Medicine, Science, and the Law, 6*(4), 200-205.

Max, L. W. (1935). Breaking up a homosexual fixation by the conditioned reaction technique: A case study. *Psychological Bulletin, 32,* 734.

Mayerson, P., & Lief, H. I. (1965). Psychotherapy of homosexuals: A follow-up study of nineteen cases. In J. Marmor (Ed.), *Sexual inversion: The multiple roots of homosexuality* (pp. 302-344). New York: Basic Books.

McConaghy, N. (1967). Penile volume change to moving pictures of male and female nudes in heterosexual and homosexual males. *Behav. Res. Therap.,* 5, 43-48.

McConaghy, N. (1969). Subjective and penile plethysmographic responses following aversion-relief and apomorphine aversion therapy for homosexual impulses. *The British Journal of Psychiatry, 115,* 723-730.

McConaghy, N. (1970). Subjective and penile plethysmograph responses to aversion therapy for homosexuality: A follow up study. *British Journal of Psychiatry, 117,* 555-560.

McConaghy, N., & Barr, R. E. (1973). Classical, avoidance and backward conditioning treatments of homosexuality. *The British Journal of Psychiatry, 122*, 151-162.

McConaghy, N., Proctor, D., & Barr, R. (1972). Subjective and penile plethysmography responses to aversion therapy for homosexuality: A partial replication. *Archives of Sexual Behavior, 2*, 65-78.

Miller, P. M., Bradley, J. B., Gross, R. S., & Wood, G. (1968). Review of homosexuality research (1960-1966) and some implications for treatment. *Psychotherapy: Theory, Research, and Practice, 5*, 3-6.

Mintz, E. (1966). Overt male homosexuals in combined group and individual treatment. *Journal of Consulting Psychology, 30*, 193-198.

Moan, C. E., & Heath, R. G. (1972). Septal stimulation for the initiation of heterosexual behavior in a homosexual male. *Journal of Behavior Therapy and Experimental Psychiatry, 3*, 23-30.

Monroe, R. R., & Enelow, R. G. (1960). The therapeutic motivation in male homosexuals. *American Journal of Psychotherapy, 14*, 474-490.

Nicolosi, J. (2003). Finally, recognition of a long-neglected population. *Archives of Sexual Behavior, 32*(5), 445-447.

Nicolosi, J., Byrd, A. D., & Potts, R. W. (2000). Retrospective self-reports of changes in homosexual orientation: A consumer survey of conversion therapy clients. *Psychological Reports, 86*, 1071-1088.

Orwin, A., James, S. R., & Turner, R. K. (1974). Sex chromosome abnormalities, homosexuality and psychological treatment. *British Journal of Psychiatry, 124*, 293-295.

Ovesey, L. (1969). *Homosexuality and pseudohomosexuality*. New York: Science House.

Ovesey, L. & Gaylin, W. (1963). Psychotherapy with male homosexuals. *American Journal of Psychotherapy, 19*, 382-396.

Ovesey, L., Gaylin, W., & Hendin, H. (1963). Psychotherapy of male homosexuality: Psychodynamic formulation. *Archives of General Psychiatry, 9*, 19-31.

Owensby, N. M. (1940). Homosexuality and lesbianism treated with Metrazol. *The Journal of Nervous and Mental Disease, 92*, 65-66.

Pattison, E. M., & Pattison, M. L. (1980). "Ex-gays": Religiously mediated change in homosexuals. *American Journal of Psychiatry, 137*, 1553-1562.

Phelan, J. E. (2013). Measuring and defining "sexual orientation": Implications for research, policy, and health care progress. Manuscript submitted for publication.

Phillips, D., Fischer, S. C., Groves, G. A., & Singh, R. (1976). Alternative behavioral approaches to the treatment of homosexuality. *Archives of Sexual Behavior, 5*, 223-228.

Pittman, F. S. III, & DeYoung, C. D. (1971). The treatment of homosexuals in heterogeneous groups. *The International Journal of Group Psychotherapy, 21*, 62-73.

Poe, J. S. (1952). The successful treatment of a 40-year-old passive homosexual based on an adaptive view of sexual behavior. *Psychoanalytic Review, 39*, 23-33.

Pomeroy, W. B. (1972). *Dr. Kinsey and The Institute for Sex Research*. New York: Harper and Row Publishers.

Pradhan, P. V., Ayyar, K. S., & Bagadia, V. N. (1982). Homosexuality: Treatment by behavior modification. *Indian Journal of Psychiatry, 24*, 80-83.

Prince, M. (1898). Sexual perversions or vice? A pathological and therapeutic inquiry. *Journal of Nervous and Mental Disease, 25*, 237-256.

Rachman, S. (1961). Sexual disorders and behavioral therapy. *American Journal of Psychiatry, 118*, 235-240.

Rado, S. (1949). An adaptive view of sexual behavior. In P. H. Hoch & J. Zubin (Eds.), *Psychosexual development in health and disease: Proceedings of the Thirty-eighth annual meeting of the American Psychopathological Association* (pp. 186-213). New York: Grune and Stratton.

Regardie, F. I. (1949). Analysis of homosexuality. *Psychiatric Quarterly, 23,* 548-566.

Rehm, L., & Rozensky, R. (1974). Multiple behavior therapy techniques with a homosexual client: A case study. *Journal of Behavioral Therapy & Experimental Psychiatry, 5,* 53-57.

Robertiello, R. C. (1959). *Voyage from lesbos: The psychoanalysis of a female homosexual.* New York: Citadel Press.

Roper, P. (1967). The effects of hypnotherapy on homosexuality. *Canadian Medical Association Journal, 96*(6), 319-327.

Rogers, C. R. & Dymond, R. F. (1954). Psychotherapy and personality change. Chicago: University of Chicago Press.

Rosik, C. H. (2003). Motivational, ethical, and epistemological foundations in the treatment of unwanted homoerotic attraction. *Journal of Marital and Family Therapy, 29,* 13-28.

Rubinstein, L. H. (1958). Psychotherapeutic aspects of male homosexuality. *British Journal of Medical Psychology, 31,* 14-18.

Schmidt, E., Castell, D., & Brown, P. (1965). A retrospective study of 42 cases of behaviour therapy. *Behaviour Research and Therapy, 3,* 9-19.

Schneider, M. S., Brown, L. S, & Glassgold, J. M. (2002). Implementing the resolution on appropriate therapeutic responses to sexual orientation: A guide for the perplexed. *Professional Psychology: Research and Practice, 3,* 265-276.

Schwartz, M. F., & Masters, W. H. (1984). The Masters and Johnson treatment program for dissatisfied homosexual men. *American Journal of Psychiatry, 141,* 173-181.

Segal, B., & Sims, J. (1972). Covert sensitization with a homosexual: A controlled replication. *Journal of Consulting and Clinical Psychology, 39,* 259-263.

Sell, R. L. (1997). Defining and measuring sexual orientation: A review. *Archives of Sexual Behavior, 26*(6), 643-658.

Serban, G. (1968). The existential therapeutic approach to homosexuality. *American Journal of Psychotherapy, 22*(3), 491-501.

Shealy, A. E. (1972). Combining behavior therapy and cognitive therapy in treating homosexuality. *Psychotherapy: Theory, Research, and Practice, 9,* 221-222.

Shidlo, A., & Schroeder, M. (2002). Changing sexual orientation: A consumer's report. *Professional Psychology: Research and Practice, 33*(3), 249-259.

Shidlo, A., Schroeder, M., & Drescher, J., (Eds.). (2001). *Sexual Conversion Therapy: Ethical, Clinical and Research Perspectives.* Binghamton, NY: The Haworth Press.

Siegel, E. V. (1988). Female homosexuality: Choice without volition: A Psychoanalytic study.

Psychoanalytic Inquiry Book Series: Vol. 9. Hilldale, NJ: The Analytic Press.

Smith, A., & Bassin, A. (1959). Overt male homosexuals in combined group and individual treatment. *Journal of Social Therapy, 5*, 225-232.

Socarides, C. W. (1968). *The overt homosexual.* New York: Grune and Stratton.

Socarides, C. W. (1978). *Homosexuality: Psychoanalytic therapy.* New York: Jason Aronson.

Socarides, C. W. & Kaufman, B. (1994). Reparative therapy [Letter]. *American Journal of Psychiatry, 115*, 157-159.

Socarides, C. W. & Kaufman, B., Nicolosi, J., Satinover, J., & Fitzgivings, R. (1997, Jan 9). Don't forsake homosexuals who want help [Letter to the editor]. *Wall Street Journal.*

Solyom, L., & Miller, S. (1965). A differential conditioning procedure as the initial phase of the behavior therapy of homosexuality. *Behaviour Research and Therapy, 3*(3), 147-160.

Spitzer, R. L. (2003). Can some gay men and lesbians change their sexual orientation? 200 participants reporting a change from homosexual to heterosexual orientation. *Archives of Sexual Behavior, 32*, 403-417.

Stekel, W. (1930). Is homosexuality curable? *Psychoanalytic Review, 17*, 443-451.

Stevens, L. (1999). Does Mental Illness Exist? Retrieved March 3, 2008, from http://www.antipsychiatry.org/exist.htm

Stevenson, I., & Wolpe, J. (1960). Recovery from sexual deviations through overcoming non-sexual neurotic responses. *American Journal of Psychiatry, 116,* 737-742.

Tanner, B. A. (1974). A comparison of automated aversive conditioning and a waiting list control in the modification of homosexual behavior in males. *Behavior Therapy, 5,* 29-32.

Tarlow, G. (1989). Clinical handbook of behavior therapy: Adult psychological disorders. Cambridge, MA: Brookline Books, Inc.

Throckmorton, W. (1998). Attempts to modify sexual orientation: A review of outcome literature and ethical issues. *Journal of Mental Health Counseling, 20,* 283-304.

TIME Dec 10, 1956 "Curable disease?"

Truax, R.A., & Tourney, G. (1971). Male homosexuals in group therapy: A controlled study. *Diseases of the Nervous System, 32*(10), 707-711.

van den Aardweg, G. J. (1971). A brief theory of homosexuality. *American Journal of Psychotherapy, 26,* 52-68.

van den Aardweg, G. J. (1986a). *Homosexuality and hope: A psychologist talks about treatment and change.* Ann Arbor, MI: Servant Books.

van den Aardweg, G. J. (1986b). *On the origins and treatment of homosexuality: A psychoanalytic reinterpretation*. New York: Praeger.

von Schrenck-Notzing, A.V. (1895). III: Sexual Paraesthesia. In Charles Gilbert Chaddock (Ed.), *Therapeutic suggestions in psychopathia sexualis (pathological manifestations of the sexual sense) with special reference to contrary sexual instinct* (pp. 117-320). London: The Davis Company.

Wallace, L. (1969). Psychotherapy of a male homosexual. *Psychoanalytic Review, 56*, 346-364.

Weinrich, J. D. & Klein, F. (2002). Bi-gay, bi-straight, and bi-bi: Three bisexual subgroups identified using cluster analysis of the Klein sexual orientation grid. *Journal of Bisexuality, 2*, 109-139.

Whitener, R., & Nikelly, A. (1964). Sexual deviation in college students. *American Journal of Orthopsychiatry, 34*, 486-492.

Wilson, G., & Davison, G. C. (1974). Behavior therapy and homosexuality: A critical perspective. *Behavior Therapy, 5*, 16-29.

Wolpe, J. (1958). Psychotherapy by reciprocal inhibition. Stanford, CA: Stanford University Press.

Woodward, M. (1958). The diagnosis and treatment of homosexual offenders: A clinical survey. *British Journal of Delinquency, 9*, 44-59.

Zucker, K. J. (2003). The politics and science of 'Reparative Therapy'. *Archives of Sexual Behavior, 32*(5), 399-402.

INDEX

NOTES/UPDATES

NOTES/UPDATES

NOTES/UPDATES